Augustine: Rejoicing in the Truth

Giants in the History of Education

Jeffrey S. Lehman, PhD

Series Editor: David Diener, PhD

Augustine: Rejoicing in the Truth

Version 1.0

ISBN: 978-1-60051-359-6

Cover and interior design template by Lenora Riley

Classical Academic Press
515 S. 32nd Street
Camp Hill, PA 17011
www.ClassicalAcademicPress.com

PGP.10.21

This book is lovingly dedicated to my wife, Jennifer, and our four children, Emily, Samantha, Jonathan, and Andrew. Daily I am reminded of God's love through their prayers, encouragement, and good cheer.

I could not hope for better companions on the journey.

People go to admire lofty mountains,
and huge breakers at sea,
and crashing waterfalls, and vast stretches
of ocean, and the dance
of the stars, but they leave themselves
behind out of sight.

Now the happy life is joy in the truth; and
that means joy in you, who are the Truth,
O God who shed the light of salvation on
my face, my God.

You pierced my heart with your Word,
and I fell in love with you.

—*Augustine,* Confessions

TABLE OF CONTENTS

ACKNOWLEDGMENTS

As I consider what made the writing of this book possible, I gratefully acknowledge my debt to many students, colleagues, friends, and family members. For nearly twenty years I have taught Augustine's *Confessions* to a wide variety of students. From classes at local parishes (St. Matthew's Church in Newport Beach, California, and St. Anthony of Padua Church in Hillsdale, Michigan) to traditional college courses (Thomas Aquinas College in Santa Paula, California, and Hillsdale College in Hillsdale, Michigan) to weeklong seminars around the country, I have been blessed with scores of bright and eager students of all ages. Each time I teach *Confessions*, my students remind me of things that I have forgotten and teach me new things that I have not seen before. I offer special thanks to the group of Hillsdale College students who took my Augustine the Teacher course in the fall of 2016. Together we read Augustine's *Confessions*, *City of God*, *On the Trinity*, and *On Christian Teaching*, along with many of his shorter works. Our conversations that year were, and have continued to be, an invaluable gift and inspiration to me.

While teaching Augustine's works, I have also benefitted from the insights of many of my colleagues. I am profoundly grateful to the late Tom Dillon, may he rest in peace, with whom I taught Augustine during my first years at Thomas Aquinas College. Tom generously shared his insights, especially on *Confessions*, and I continue to benefit from what he taught me about how to read this book (as well as so many others). Another dear friend and colleague, Steve Smith of Hillsdale College, has been an excellent dialogue partner since our graduate school days at the University of Dallas; we have spent countless hours talking about Augustine, *and* Dante, *and* Shakespeare, *and* Plato. A kindred spirit and kind man, Steve has influenced my thinking more than I can reckon on Augustine and on countless other matters. Finally, Gerry Wegemer of the University of Dallas has been a constant source of wisdom and encouragement in my studies of Augustine.

Others have supported and encouraged this project in significant ways: Mary Catherine Adams, David Arias, Mike Augros, Ben Beier, Chris Blum, Dan Coupland, Peter Cross, Daryl Glick, Kirstin Kiledal, Ken Larson, Clarke Mitchell, Fr. David Reamsnyder, Sarah Rinaldi, Andrew Seeley, Emily Sullivan, and Karen Zedlick. I am deeply grateful to Emily Lehman, Morgan Brownfield, Peter Cross, Samantha Lehman, Clarke Mitchell, and Dani Ruedisueli, who read all or part of the manuscript.

Richard Gamble kindly recommended me to write this volume, and David Diener has been a delight to work with as series editor. Many thanks to him and the entire editorial staff at Classical Academic Press.

Finally, I offer a special thanks to my wife, Jennifer, and our children, Emily, Samantha, Jonathan, and Andrew. Their understanding and encouragement along the way have made this project a joy.

Introduction

If one were to make a short list of those who have had the greatest influence on education in the Greco-Roman and Judeo-Christian traditions, undoubtedly Augustine's name would be near the top. Setting aside Plato and Aristotle, few others have made such a profound and enduring impression upon the theory and practice of education in the West prior to the twentieth century. Augustine was the first Christian to offer a detailed account of the liberal arts and their proper place in a liberal education, and much of what we take to be the traditional understanding of classical education is due at least in part to his early synthesis. Indeed, the general plan of studies, beginning with the liberal arts and proceeding to the various disciplines and ultimately to philosophy and theology, was championed by Augustine and handed down through the Middle Ages to the modern period. This plan of studies was the nearly universal standard for education in the West until well into the nineteenth century.

From an early age, Augustine was an ardent seeker of truth, unflinchingly pursuing it wherever he thought it might be found. Yet, for all his seeking after truth, Augustine ultimately became convinced that it was rather the Truth that had been seeking him. In striving to know himself, Augustine came to realize that self-knowledge is only possible through a knowledge of God, who subsists eternally as a Trinity of Persons in loving communion with one another. In searching for the truth, Augustine opened himself up to the God who *is* Truth (John 14:6); and the God who is Truth is also the God who is Love (1 John 4:8). Pursued by his divine lover, Augustine came to see that human happiness is attainable only through loving communion with God. In the end, he tells us, "There shall be one Christ loving himself"—Christ the Head united to his Body, the Church, for all eternity.[1] Thus, for Augustine, all education is ultimately ordered to a knowledge and love of God (and of one's neighbor, for God's sake). In the pages that follow, we will unfold Augustine's philosophy and theology of education, outlining his account of how one comes to know the truth and to love the truth.

In the first two chapters of this book, the stage is set through a brief biography (chapter 1) and an exploration of Augustine's historical and intellectual context (chapter 2). Chapter 3 provides an overview of his understanding of the nature and purpose of education, beginning with his earliest philosophical dialogues and noting how his understanding had developed by the time he wrote his later works. In chapter 4, we will consider Augustine's account of the liberal arts and liberal education, identifying how these may be conducive to man's pursuit of happiness. Chapter 5 illustrates the evidence of Augustine's theory and practice of education in his writings as a master teacher. In the final chapter, our study concludes with a look at Augustine's legacy and relevance today.

---

1. Augustine, "Tenth Homily," in *Homilies on the First Epistle of John*, trans. Boniface Ramsey, vol. 14 of *The Works of St. Augustine* (Hyde Park, NY: New City Press, 2008), 148. This passage contains an excellent summary of Augustine's doctrine of the *totus Christus*, or "whole Christ," demonstrating the centrality of love to his understanding of man's ultimate end. See, for example, pages 147–148:

> [T]he sons of God are the body of the only son of God, and, since he is the head and we are the members, the Son of God is one. Therefore, he who loves the sons of God loves the Son of God, and he who loves the Son of God loves the Father. Nor can anyone love the Father unless he loves the Son, and he who loves the Son also loves the sons of God. Which sons of God? The members of the Son of God. And he himself also becomes a member by loving, and through love he comes to be in the structure of Christ's body, and there shall be one Christ loving himself. For, when the members love each other, the body loves itself.

CHAPTER ONE
St. Augustine of Hippo: A Life in Brief

Writing a biographical sketch of an ancient figure can be daunting. Often the difficulty arises from the meager knowledge we have of biographical details, but with St. Augustine of Hippo (AD 354–430), the opposite is the case. Of all authors from antiquity, we know more about the life of Augustine than perhaps that of any other figure. First, of course, we possess his *Confessions*, a masterpiece of Western literature in which Augustine gives an account of his own life from "first beginnings" (*primordia*) up to the time of his conversion in 387. Then, we have the *Life of St. Augustine*, penned by Possidius of Calama, a close friend and fellow bishop who wrote the text to inform his readers of Augustine's later life as a presbyter and bishop. While Possidius's *Vita* is an "affectionate portrait of a friend and mentor," it also provides a detailed account of Augustine's public life from his conversion to his death in 430.[1] Finally, in addition to *Confessions* we possess a staggeringly large treasury of Augustine's writings: from his early philosophical dialogues, such as *Against the Academic Skeptics* and *On the Happy Life*; to weighty treatises, such as *City of God* and *On the Trinity*; to biblical commentaries, such as

1. Anthony P. Schiavo Jr., "Preface to the 2008 Edition," in Possidius, *The Life of St. Augustine: A Translation of the* Sancti Augustini Vita *by Possidius, Bishop of Calama*, trans. Herbert T. Weiskotten, vol. 6 of *Christian Roman Empire Series* (Merchantville, NJ: Evolution Publishing, 2008), iii. In his preface to the *Vita*, Possidius identifies his purpose in writing:

> Inspired by God, the Maker and Ruler of all, and mindful of my purpose wherein through the grace of the Savior I resolved faithfully to serve the omnipotent and divine Trinity . . . I am eager with whatever ability and eloquence I possess, to aid in the edification of the holy and true Catholic Church of Christ our Lord, and so [have resolved] not to keep silent concerning the life and character of the most noble bishop Augustine, predestined long ago and presented in his own time—the things that I have seen in him and heard from him.

This passage makes evident the extent to which Possidius had imbibed the teaching of his friend and mentor.

his multiple works on the book of Genesis and his "Expositions" (*Enarrationes*) of the Psalms; to his polemical writings, such as *On Baptism* (a reply to the Donatists) and *On Nature and Grace* (a response to the Pelagians); to nearly three hundred letters and four hundred sermons (excluding those delivered as serial commentaries on biblical books). Altogether, Augustine's literary corpus runs to over 5.4 million words.[2] What is more, even today the extant body of his writings continues to grow.[3] Clearly, then, we suffer from no lack of material. In light of this embarrassment of riches, the principal task of the author of a brief biography becomes deciding what to leave out. What follows is a modest outline of the major stages of Augustine's life, highlighting the most salient features of his moral and intellectual development insofar as they shed light on his mature philosophy and theology of education.

Augustine's Birth and Early Life (354–373)

Aurelius Augustinus[4] was born on November 13, 354, in the small municipality of Thagaste (modern-day Souk Ahras, Algeria) in Numidia, one of seven Roman provinces in Africa. At the time of Augustine's birth, his mother, Monica, was a devout (if not

2. To put this unwieldy number into perspective, if this corpus were printed in volumes containing 250 pages each, with 300 words per page, the collected works would fill over 72 volumes! Among the extant works other than *Confessions*, many of the most valuable biographical details are found in his sermons and letters.
3. For example, in 1969, Johannes Divjak, a Viennese scholar working in a library in Marseille, France, discovered a collection of letters that contained twenty-nine epistles of Augustine previously unknown to modern scholars. Then, in 1990, François Dolbeau, a French scholar conducting research in a library in Mainz, Germany, was studying a medieval volume of sermons and found twenty-six homilies by Augustine that had been recorded by Possidius in his *indiculus* (or "list") of Augustine's collected works but were also unknown to modern scholars. Finally, as recently as 2008, three scholars from the Austrian Academy of Science found six additional previously undiscovered sermons of Augustine in a research library at the University of Erfurt, Germany.
4. It was Roman custom to place the family name first, followed by the given name.

yet well-catechized) Christian; his father, Patricius, was a worldly, ambitious pagan. In the desires and aspirations of his parents, we see in microcosm the tension that existed in the Roman world of late antiquity, a tension between the centuries-old Roman way of life with its civic religion and the relatively new Christian faith that transcended the limits of space and time and required allegiance to a king and kingdom not of this world. Patricius was a *curialis*, a minor city official who came from a traditional Roman family committed to traditional Roman ways. Though Augustine is discreet in speaking about the matter, it is clear that Patricius was not faithful to his long-suffering wife. Nor in these years was Patricius at all interested in her religion, which he likely perceived to be an innovative superstition at odds with traditional Roman religion. For her part, Monica did her best to commend her Christian faith to Augustine, albeit with fairly minimal success in the early years. At his birth, Augustine was "signed with the cross and given his salt,"[5] ritualistic signs of being initiated into the catechumenate of the Catholic faith. Even so, during his childhood when Augustine was "seized by stomach pains and . . . came near to death,"[6] Monica decided not to have Augustine baptized once he made a rapid recovery. As Augustine tells the story of his childhood, "reading" the character of his parents, they are images—however imperfect—of the two cities: his mother representing the City of God, his father the Earthly City.[7]

Augustine's parents made significant sacrifices to obtain the best education they could afford for their son. Central to this education was the study of rhetoric, or oratory. In the Roman world at the time, becoming a master of rhetoric was the most reliable route to social and political advancement. From 365 to 369, Augustine spent his first years away from home in Madaura (now M'Daourouch, Algeria) studying

5. Augustine, *The Confessions of Saint Augustine of Hippo*, trans. Maria Boulding, OSB, ed. David Vincent Meconi, SJ, Ignatius Critical Editions (San Francisco: Ignatius Press, 2012), 1.11.17. Unless otherwise indicated, all quotations of *Confessions* are from this edition.

6. Augustine, 1.11.17.

7. Augustine, 2.3.8.

"grammar" (Latin literature).[8] After this, Augustine returned home for a year to save up money for additional education. He then traveled to Carthage, where he studied rhetoric from 370 to 373. Although not always the model student, Augustine excelled in his studies, eventually receiving an invitation to serve as the imperial rhetor in Milan, the capital of the Western Roman Empire at the time.

In the desires and aspirations of his parents, we see in microcosm the tension that existed in the Roman world of late antiquity, a tension between the centuries-old Roman way of life with its civic religion and the relatively new Christian faith that transcended the limits of space and time and required allegiance to a king and kingdom not of this world.

During "the customary course of study" in the art of rhetoric, Augustine came across Cicero's *Hortensius*, an exhortation to the philosophical way of life. Augustine describes his encounter with *Hortensius* as bringing about a "conversion" of mind and heart:

> The book changed my way of feeling and the character of my prayers to you, O Lord, for under its influence my petitions and desires altered. All my hollow hopes [i.e., for worldly advancement] suddenly seemed worthless, and with unbelievable intensity my heart burned with longing for the immortality that wisdom seemed to promise. I began to rise up, in order to return to you [cf. Luke 15:18-20].[9]

Significantly, reading this text initiated a turning of Augustine's mind to the pursuit of wisdom and a turning of his heart to ever-higher objects of love. For Augustine, the pursuit of wisdom

8. Augustine, 1.9.14.
9. Augustine, 3.4.7.

is able—at least in part—to reorder one's desires; as one grows in knowledge of the truth, one comes to love those things that are most inherently worthy of love. And as his allusion to the parable of the prodigal son indicates, the ultimate object of Augustine's love becomes God, who subsists eternally in a Trinity of Persons: Father, Son, and Holy Spirit.

Another important effect of Augustine's reading of *Hortensius* was a growing awareness that education must be ordered to more than simply eloquence: "My interest in the book was not aroused by its usefulness in the honing of verbal skills (which was supposed to be the object of the studies I was now pursuing) . . . no, it was not merely as an instrument for sharpening my tongue that I used that book, for it had won me over not by its style but by what it had to say."[10] The relation of wisdom and eloquence and their place in education would become central themes in Augustine's writings.

For Augustine, the pursuit of wisdom is able—at least in part—to reorder one's desires; as one grows in knowledge of the truth, one comes to love those things that are most inherently worthy of love. And as his allusion to the parable of the prodigal son indicates, the ultimate object of Augustine's love becomes God, who subsists eternally in a Trinity of Persons: Father, Son, and Holy Spirit.

His reading of *Hortensius* also gave rise to Augustine's resolve to make the pursuit of truth a way of life: "I was aroused and kindled

10. Augustine, 3.4.7.

and set on fire to love and seek and capture and hold fast and strongly cling not to this or that school, but to wisdom itself, whatever it might be."[11] Armed with this resolve, Augustine turned first to the Christian Scriptures. Regrettably, however, he was still too filled with intellectual pride to acknowledge the truth when it was not accompanied by eloquence: "When I studied the Bible and compared it with Cicero's dignified prose, it seemed to me unworthy."[12] Unwilling to accept the unadorned truth of Scripture, Augustine was quickly ensnared by a then-popular gnostic religion: Manichaeism.

Manichean Wanderings (373–383)

Named after its founder, Mani, a Persian mystic who lived from roughly 215 to 276, Manichaeism taught that there are two fundamental principles of reality: one supremely good (*summum bonum*) and the other supremely evil (*summum malum*). When these "deities" came into conflict with one another, they became intermingled, which resulted in the visible, material world coming into being. The world as we now experience it, Manichees argued, is a mixture of irreconcilable opposites: light and darkness, good and evil, spirit and matter, male and female. Since neither the good principle nor the evil principle can overcome its opponent, there is an inevitable dualism in the cosmos. Thus, the average person cannot hope to live free from the never-ending war between good and evil. Only a select few, those privy to the "secret" knowledge passed down through the teachings of Mani, could be delivered from this dualistic dilemma.

Adherents of Manichean religion were divided into the "elect" and the "hearers." The first were those who could liberate the good

11. Augustine, 3.4.8.
12. Augustine, 3.5.9.

deity from its bondage within material objects. Since sexual intercourse necessarily involves the body, the elect refrained from sexual relations so as not to perpetuate the entrapment of the good spirit in material (and thus evil) bodies. The inferior class of "hearers" performed a daily routine of prayers and served this elite class in various ways, such as by providing them with fruits and vegetables to chew in order to release the principle of good from its incarceration in matter. Significantly, the Manicheans presented their religion as a purified form of Christianity, a religion within the limits of reason alone. They ridiculed traditional Christian belief and openly attacked the Old Testament on the grounds that its depiction of God was anthropomorphic and its morality barbaric.

Augustine was a hearer among the Manichees for nine years. What appealed to him in this strange gnostic sect? First of all, it offered a rational response to the problem of evil, a problem that deeply troubled Augustine prior to his conversion to Christianity. Living during the eclipse of the Western Roman Empire, Augustine witnessed firsthand abundant evidence of evil and suffering in the world. If there is a God, and he knows about evil and has the power to prevent it, why doesn't he do so? A philosopher might formulate the question this way: Given the existence of an omniscient, omnipotent God, whence comes evil? The Manichean response to the problem of evil was simply to deny God's omnipotence. This response "solves" the problem in a rational way, even if it does so at the expense of God's ability to administer justice. Even more appealing to Augustine was the way that Manichaeism removed moral responsibility for one's own actions. Clearly, if there are two irreconcilable principles at war in every human heart, man cannot be held responsible for what he does.

Among his other moral failings, Augustine tells us that he struggled for years with sexual sin. During his period of study in Carthage (370–373), Augustine met a young woman and had intimate relations with her as a concubine for many years.

One result of this union was the birth of Augustine's son, named Adeodatus ("given by God"). Although the Manichean elect were required to take a vow of celibacy, no such burden was placed upon hearers. Given the no-fault theodicy championed by the Manichean religion, Augustine was content to allow this and other sins—especially intellectual pride—to fester.

Eventually, however, Augustine became disillusioned with Manichaeism. For all his acknowledged faults during this period of his life, Augustine never lost his passion for truth. In fact, one of the initial reasons Augustine had thrown in his lot with the Manichees was that they claimed to adhere to a thoroughly rational religion, one involving no appeal to faith, authority, or anything beyond what a reasonable person could readily accept. Alongside a creed based upon a "purged" version of Christianity, the Manichees claimed to have an entire cosmology that coincided with and reinforced their theology. Having been a student of the liberal arts himself, Augustine was well aware of the current teachings of philosophers and astronomers regarding the nature of the heavens. This led Augustine to question many of the cosmological claims made by the Manichees. The standard response to his questions was that Augustine must wait for Faustus, a Manichean bishop reputed to be "extremely well informed . . . in all branches of reputable scholarship, and . . . particularly learned in the liberal arts."[13] When Faustus arrived in 383, however, Augustine was deeply disappointed: "What I found was a man ill-educated in the liberal arts, apart from grammar, and even in that schooled only to an average level."[14] When Augustine finally was able to pose his questions, "[Faustus] refused courteously enough, reluctant to risk taking on that burden; for he knew that he did not know about these matters, and was not ashamed to admit it."[15] After this encounter with Faustus, Augustine

13. Augustine, 5.3.3.
14. Augustine, 5.6.11.
15. Augustine, 5.7.12.

lost all hope of finding the truth in the Manichean religion. For a brief period, he entertained the possibility that he should resign himself to skepticism, ever searching for the truth but having no serious prospect of finding it.

Bishop Ambrose and the Books of the Platonists (383–387)

After briefly operating his own school of grammar, rhetoric, and dialectic back in Thagaste (374–376), and then returning to Carthage and finding considerable success as a teacher and practitioner of rhetoric, Augustine decided in 383 to move to Rome in order to begin a new career teaching rhetoric. The principal reason for the move, from his perspective, was to teach students who were more docile and well behaved than his students had been in Carthage. Augustine quickly found, however, that his hope for better students in Rome would not be realized. Although he was frustrated by this at the time, in retrospect he saw God's "deep, secret providence" as well as his "ever-present mercy" at work,[16] for in 384 he was summoned to Milan to serve as imperial rhetor. He also finally broke all ties with the Manichees, and he met Ambrose, bishop of Milan, "who was known throughout the world as one of the best of men."[17] The following year, his mother, Monica, arrived in Milan. Then, in 386, Augustine read the "books of the Platonists" and began to understand how to interpret the Christian Scriptures aright. Of all the aforementioned events, two stand out as particularly significant for Augustine's moral and intellectual formation. The first is his meeting Ambrose and the lessons he learned from observing the bishop's character and teachings. The

16. Augustine, 5.8.14.
17. Augustine, 5.13.23.

second is his reading the books of the Platonists and the intellectual conversion that these books precipitated.

The life and teachings of Ambrose made a deep and lasting impression on Augustine, who saw their meeting as ordained by God to bring him to the Catholic faith: "Unknowingly I was led by you [God] to him [Ambrose], so that through him I might be led, knowingly, to you." Indeed, to Augustine, Ambrose was a spiritual father, a "man of God who welcomed [Augustine] with fatherly kindness and showed the charitable concern for [his] pilgrimage that befitted a bishop."[18] Initially, Augustine went only to hear the rhetoric of Ambrose's sermons; he had heard of the man's eloquence and wanted to experience it for himself. When he first went to listen, he despised the message itself, having no real expectation of discovering truth in the Christian faith. Nevertheless, Augustine found himself moved by the content of Ambrose's sermons as well: "As his words, which I enjoyed, penetrated my mind, the substance, which I overlooked, seeped in with them, for I could not separate the two."[19]

Ambrose's manifest virtue and remarkable discipline were humbling to Augustine. Whereas Augustine had involved himself in the self-absorbed pursuit of his own worldly success, Ambrose had renounced the world and given himself unreservedly to serving his Christian flock. Whereas Augustine had used his eloquence to rise to a position of prominence and prestige in the imperial court, Ambrose had employed his eloquence to admonish the faithful and encourage them to lead holy lives. Finally, whereas Augustine had resolved so many years prior to follow the truth wherever it might lead, and yet had failed to follow through on his resolution, Ambrose had disciplined himself in the pursuit of truth through moral and intellectual virtue, embodying the love of truth that Augustine had by now all but abandoned.

18. Augustine, 5.13.23.
19. Augustine, 5.14.24.

Beyond all this, Ambrose taught Augustine how to read the Bible with prudence and profit. Introducing Augustine to allegorical interpretation, Ambrose made clear to Augustine that not every passage and word of the Bible is meant to be interpreted literally:

> I delighted to hear Ambrose often asserting in his sermons to the people, as a principle on which he must insist emphatically, *The letter is death-dealing, but the spirit gives life* [2 Corinthians 3:6]. This he would tell them as he drew aside the veil of mystery and opened to them the spiritual meaning of passages which, taken literally, would seem to mislead.[20]

This principle of interpretation enabled Augustine to dispel the specious arguments of the Manichees against the theology and morality of the Old Testament. It also prepared him to understand more fully what it means for man to be made in the image and likeness of God (Genesis 1:26-27).

Another significant event during this period was Augustine's reading of the "books of the Platonists." While in Milan, Augustine was introduced to the writings of Plotinus (204–270), a Neoplatonic philosopher born in Egypt who later established a very successful school of philosophy in Rome. Plotinus reflected upon and developed many of the central teachings of Plato for his own generation. His student Porphyry (ca. 232–303) then collected and organized Plotinus's writings into a whole called the *Enneads*. Augustine's reading of this work transformed his understanding of both the nature of God and the nature of evil. Regarding God, Augustine came to embrace the possibility of immaterial being. Having struggled for years to comprehend God as some sort of grand material being, Augustine followed the advice of the Neoplatonists to "seek for truth beyond corporeal forms" and to "turn [his] gaze toward [God's] invisible reality."[21]

---

20. Augustine, 6.4.6.

21. See Augustine, 7.20.26.

This was a crucial step in Augustine's conversion to Christianity, as it helped him see that, ultimately, the best of rational philosophy and rightly understood Christian faith complement one another. The "books of the Platonists" also gave Augustine a new understanding of evil. For Plotinus, all that exists is good; therefore, evil must be a "privation" of the good. In other words, there is no "principle of evil," as the Manichees had taught. Instead, evil is a lack of some sort in a being that is by nature good. The implications of this view of evil were tremendous for Augustine, leading in time to his confession that the evils of his past and present thoughts, words, and deeds were his own responsibility.

Conversion and Beyond (387–430)

Since much of Augustine's life following his conversion will be discussed in later chapters, the treatment here will be relatively brief. Following his encounter with the books of the Platonists in the early winter of 386, Augustine had his famous conversion experience in the garden of Milan[22] and resigned from his position as professor of rhetoric. He then retired to a villa in Cassiciacum (north of Milan) with his mother, his son, and a few friends in order to prepare for baptism. Their retreat lasted from November 386 through March 387, and Augustine based his "Cassiciacum

22. See Augustine, 8.8.19–12.29. Briefly, Augustine's experience in the garden of Milan was as follows. Having reached a moment of crisis, Augustine and his friend Alypius are in the garden. Augustine longs for the peace of conversion, but he still wavers due to lingering attachment to habitual sins of the flesh. While some distance away from Alypius, Augustine hears a child's voice say, "Take up and read" (*Tolle lege*). He takes up a collection of St. Paul's writings and reads Romans 13:13-14, which exhorts readers to "put on the Lord Jesus Christ" and "make no provision for the flesh." Reading these verses and applying them to himself, Augustine is filled with complete confidence and all uncertainty is dispelled. He returns to tell Alypius, who reads the next line (Romans 14:1) about accepting the one who is weak in faith. Alypius applies this verse to himself, and the two friends surrender themselves to God's will and purpose for them.

dialogues" upon their conversations during this time. Augustine and the other catechumens were baptized by Bishop Ambrose at the Easter Vigil Mass on April 24, 387. Later that spring, Monica died in Ostia, shortly after sharing a mystical vision with Augustine as they overlooked a garden.[23] In 388, Augustine returned to Thagaste with his son, Adeodatus, to found a monastic community dedicated to prayer, study, and manual labor.

Augustine's attempt at living a monastic life was cut short when in 391 he was ordained a Catholic priest for the diocese of Hippo Regius by Bishop Valerius. Four years later he was consecrated as an auxiliary bishop alongside Valerius, who died shortly thereafter. Augustine remained bishop of Hippo Regius until his death. In 428, Augustine sat down with his faithful secretary and friend, Possidius, and composed *Retractationes* (*Revisions*), which chronicles and summarizes all of Augustine's written works and occasionally offers additional comments or corrections.

In 429 Gaiseric and his Vandal army descended through the Straits of Gibraltar into North Africa, arriving on the outskirts of Hippo the following year to lay siege to the city. Perhaps due to the intercession of Augustine, the town of Hippo was spared complete destruction and Augustine's library survived essentially intact. Augustine contracted a high fever, however, likely due to malaria, and died in the bishop's residence on August 28, 430.[24]

In the concluding chapter of his *Life of St. Augustine*, Possidius makes the following comments about the man with whom he had lived and ministered "on terms of intimate and delightful friendship, with no bitter disagreement, for almost forty years":

> From [Augustine's] writing it is manifest that this priest, beloved and acceptable to God, lived

---

23. Augustine, 9.10.23–26.

24. According to Possidius, before Augustine became too ill, he had the penitential psalms copied and posted on the wall of his bedroom so that he could pray and meditate upon them during his final hours.

> uprightly and soberly in the faith, hope and love of the Catholic Church in so far as he was permitted to see it by the light of truth, and those who read his works on divine subjects profit thereby. But I believe that they were able to derive greater good from him who heard and saw him as he spoke in person in the church, and especially those who knew well his manner of life among men.[25]

Contemporary biographies of Augustine abound. For all their merits, these accounts typically shy away from presenting the genuine virtues of this great man. Possidius, on the other hand, a man who knew Augustine intimately, had the courage and humility to bear testimony to Augustine's character. A teacher among teachers, Augustine's life embodied the truths he taught in his writings. Although we do not have the privilege of knowing Augustine personally as Possidius did, we nevertheless can search Augustine's writings in order to discern his philosophy and theology of education, and to follow his example of living uprightly and soberly in faith, hope, and love.

25. Possidius, *The Life of St. Augustine*, 31.

Chapter Two

Augustine's World: Historical and Intellectual Context

Any age of human history is at odds with itself in significant ways. Various trends of thought and action pull in different directions, challenging the status quo and putting strain on any existing economic, political, and ideological stability. Even with these challenges, there is typically enough continuity for the age to persist in a way that is discernible from the historian's point of view. On other occasions, however, the tension between the old ways and the new comes to a point of crisis, bringing about a fundamental change in the established order. The Roman world of late antiquity, the world of Augustine, was a time of widespread and momentous transition, a period when the old order of pagan antiquity was giving way to what would eventually become medieval Christendom and the new unity we call Europe. As mentioned in the first chapter, Augustine's own family embodied this tension and this transition, given his father's Roman paganism and his mother's commitment to Christianity.

The Roman world of late antiquity, the world of Augustine, was a time of widespread and momentous transition, a period when the old order of pagan antiquity was giving way to what would eventually become medieval Christendom and the new unity we call Europe.

Before proceeding, we need to note how very "Roman" the North Africa of Augustine's lifetime really was. There have been scholars in recent years who have made a great deal—too much, it would seem—of Augustine as an "African." This view fails to account for the profound way Roman civilization had taken root throughout the empire, including in the Roman provinces of Africa. Ryan N. S. Topping sums it up well:

> By Augustine's time, Roman North Africa had enjoyed the benefits of empire for several hundred years. United in prosperity and by culture, in a significant way in the fourth century Rome was Athens was Carthage. Educated people read the same books. They shared the same philosophical ideas. And they were awarded similar privileges. Augustine's African birth did not separate him from Greco-Roman civilization. He was steeped in the common rhetorical and philosophical tradition of Latin late antiquity that looked back, among others, to Cicero, to Virgil, and to Varro. By the time of his birth . . . Augustine's family had been Roman for a century and a half.[1]

Notwithstanding his mother Monica's purported Berber origins, Augustine was a Roman of Roman stock. He received a liberal education grounded in the greatest Roman authors, and even in his native North Africa he lived in a world that had been dominated by Roman ways of life for generations. Before his conversion to Christianity, Augustine thought like a Roman, taught like a Roman, and engaged in social and political life like any typical Roman man would have done. Furthermore, after his conversion Augustine did not simply repudiate his Roman past. Evidence of his indebtedness to his Greco-Roman education is abundantly present in Augustine's early postconversion writings, the Cassiciacum dialogues. His more mature works likewise bear

1. Ryan N. S. Topping, *St. Augustine, Continuum Library of Educational Thought* (New York: Continuum International Publishing Group, 2010), 4.

the marks of his reliance upon and response to the greatest of his Roman teachers: Cicero, Virgil, and Varro. In these later works, Augustine does not so much renounce his Roman heritage as he transforms it in light of the Christian gospel.

Augustine was a Roman of Roman stock. He received a liberal education grounded in the greatest Roman authors, and even in his native North Africa he lived in a world that had been dominated by Roman ways of life for generations. Before his conversion to Christianity, Augustine thought like a Roman, taught like a Roman, and engaged in social and political life like any typical Roman man would have done.

The "Great Persecution" and Its Aftermath

Returning to the general topic of the tension between the established ways of pagan Rome and the new beliefs of Christianity, a few significant events help us to more fully understand Augustine and his world. Beginning with Jesus Christ and his twelve apostles, who were sent out as the first Christian missionaries in the middle of the first century AD, the Christian faith steadily grew in numbers as well as in political strength throughout the Roman world.[2] Current estimates indicate that by 250 there were approximately one million Christians living in the empire. Contrary to

2. My account of the growth of Christianity in this paragraph is indebted to Rodney Stark's *The Rise of Christianity: A Sociologist Reconsiders History* (Princeton: Princeton University Press, 1996).

long-standing legend, Christianity was *not* principally a movement of the downtrodden, a religion for Roman slaves and the impoverished rural masses. Instead, the Christian faith took root and grew most rapidly in major metropolitan areas, and it was particularly successful among the middle and upper classes, which consisted largely of established and often influential Roman citizens. The new religion was so successful, in fact, that by 300 the number of Christians in the empire had swelled to roughly six million.

Not surprisingly, this upstart religion from Palestine came to be perceived by many traditionally minded Romans as a threat to the established political order. Although there had been intermittent periods of persecution since the founding of the Christian faith, the "Great Persecution" of 303 was the last and most severe in antiquity. Instigated by the Roman emperor Diocletian, it was a widespread and systematic attempt to exterminate Christians entirely. Often on pain of death, Christians were ordered to renounce their faith and comply with the traditional practices of Roman civic religion. As a sign of their submission to the persecutors' demands, priests and bishops were required to hand over their copies of the Christian Scriptures, the sacred vessels used in the celebration of the Eucharist, and the names of other Christians who had not yet obeyed the imperial edict. Those who refused to do so were imprisoned, or in some cases tortured and martyred. The period of persecution was most acute from 303 to 305. When Constantine took imperial office in 306, he alleviated the suffering of Christians and began to dismantle the apparatus of state-imposed persecution. The period of persecution officially ended in 313 with the Edict of Milan, which formally restored legal status to Christians and, to the extent possible, restored their confiscated property.

As welcome as the end of the "Great Persecution" no doubt was, it also presented difficult questions for the Christians who had survived it. What would become of the character of Christianity now that fierce political opposition from Rome had been removed? Given that religious freedom had been granted, how should Christians think about the relation of their faith to the current political order—or to *any* political order, for that matter? Another difficult question centered on what should be done about those who had capitulated to the demands of their persecutors. Priests and bishops who had given in to the persecution came to be known as *traditores*, that is, those who "handed over" the Scriptures, the sacred vessels, and the names of fellow believers. Could the *traditores* ever be trusted again? Even more pointedly, had they forfeited their right to serve as priests and bishops by publicly renouncing the Christian faith under pressure?

As welcome as the end of the "Great Persecution" no doubt was, it also presented difficult questions for the Christians who had survived it. What would become of the character of Christianity now that fierce political opposition from Rome had been removed?

In the course of his life, Augustine responded to each of these questions. We will address his thoughts on the relation of the Church to secular political power in chapter 5 when we discuss his *City of God*. For now, let us focus on the more particular questions about the *traditores*.

Throughout Augustine's life, Christians in North Africa were sharply divided over how to respond to these questions. On one side were the Donatists, named after Donatus, one of the first bishops of the separatist group. They held that anyone who had lapsed during the persecution was *ipso facto* cut off from the Church. Simply by virtue of the fact that these clerics had become *traditores*, both their baptisms and their ordinations were deemed automatically annulled.

Donatists believed that there was a necessary connection between the virtue of a clergyman and the validity of the sacraments he administered. Put simply, bad men cannot administer efficacious sacraments. Catholics, on the other hand, denied this necessary connection between the virtue of the clergyman and the validity of the sacrament. To them, the efficacy of a sacrament was completely and exclusively secured through the finished work of Christ (*ex opere operato*—that is, "out of the work already worked"). Thus, while an ordained minister is the divinely appointed means of administering the sacrament, his personal sanctity (or lack thereof) has no bearing whatsoever on the efficacy of the sacrament, provided that it is administered in the way that has been handed down from the apostles, who received it from Christ himself.

Tensions between Donatists and Catholics in North Africa were common and at times very fierce. As an ordained bishop, Augustine took part in a major council at Carthage in 411 to respond to the conflict. Defending the Catholic position, he debated this issue with a Donatist opponent before the assembled council. Although the imperial magistrate at the council ruled in favor of the Catholics, the Donatists continued to be an antagonistic presence in North Africa until the Muslim invasions of the eighth century.

Augustine's efforts in speaking and writing against the Donatists are an illustrative example of how he responded to the tensions and transitions of his time. Having grown up in a world in which traditional Roman pagans were at odds with Christians, and Christians themselves were in conflict with one another, Augustine faithfully served as a teacher and ecclesial leader. Throughout his life as a bishop, he responded in a timely and effective manner to challenges from within the Christian faith as well as from outside forces. Influenced by the historical, political, and ecclesial realities of his time, he influenced them in turn, bringing clear-headed reasoning and prudent action to bear upon the problems of his age.

Orators, Philosophers, and the Bible

In addition to the historical context of Augustine's world, we should also consider his intellectual context. In what remains of this chapter, my purpose is twofold. First, I want to outline two distinct branches within the Western tradition of education: what have come to be called the rhetorical tradition (the "Orators") and the philosophical tradition (the "Philosophers").[3] Second, I want to draw attention to what was undoubtedly the greatest influence on Augustine's thinking in the years leading up to and following his conversion: the Bible.

Essentially, two distinct schools of thought on the nature and purpose of education have developed in the Western tradition. The rhetorical tradition, championed by Isocrates (436–338 BC) and his disciples through the ages, focuses on the cultivation of the art of rhetoric and the public performance of this art. For the Orator, education's ultimate goal is to prepare students to take their place as productive, responsible members of society who are able to engage in public discourse, to take an active part in political deliberation, and to contribute thereby to the good of the regime. The philosophical tradition, championed by Socrates (ca. 470–399 BC), Plato (ca. 428–348 BC), and their disciples, principally employs dialectic and is ordered to the discovery of truth. For the Philosopher, the unfettered pursuit of truth is the ultimate purpose of education. There is a strong emphasis in this tradition on knowledge for its own sake. While the distinction between the rhetorical and philosophical traditions can be overstated, they are nonetheless distinct approaches to education within the Western tradition, approaches that avail themselves of different texts and different pedagogies in order to educate their students.

3. For a detailed treatment of these two branches and their interactions throughout the Western tradition, see Bruce A. Kimball's *Orators and Philosophers: A History of the Idea of Liberal Education* (New York: Teachers College Press, 1986).

Augustine's early training in grammar and rhetoric was decidedly within the rhetorical tradition. His reading of Cicero and other authors of rhetorical treatises, as well as the speaking exercises and contests he describes in *Confessions*, are clear evidence of this. Nevertheless, Augustine's intellectual journey as recounted in *Confessions* bears testimony to the fact that as he developed intellectually, he became more and more committed to the philosophical tradition. Abundant evidence of this will come to light when we discuss some of his works in detail in later chapters. For the moment, it is sufficient to know about these two different branches and to realize that his own philosophy and theology became less indebted to the rhetorical tradition as he matured.

His encounters with Sacred Scripture over the years had a profound and enduring influence on the way he thought as well as on the way he taught. Philosophy itself had to be reconsidered in light of the truths of the Christian faith.

Finally, we must remind ourselves of what is obvious to readers with any prior exposure to Augustine's life and writings—namely that throughout the more than four decades after his conversion during which Augustine taught and wrote, the Bible was far and away the most significant influence on his philosophy and theology of education. His encounters with Sacred Scripture over the years had a profound and enduring influence on the way he thought as well as on the way he taught. Philosophy itself had to be reconsidered in light of the truths of the Christian faith. For this reason alone, any attempt to write an account of Augustine's *philosophy* of education without taking into consideration his *theology* of education is doomed to failure.

Chapter Three

Rejoicing in the Truth: On the Nature and Purpose of Education

Augustine's account of the ultimate purpose of education falls within the "eudaimonist" tradition. That is to say, for Augustine the final goal of all teaching and learning is happiness, or human flourishing (Greek *eudaimonia*; Latin *beatitudo*), a state of being that is inherently desirable and that amounts to the perfection of human nature achieved through the practice of moral and intellectual virtue. Plato, Aristotle, the Epicureans, and the Stoics all defended versions of eudaimonism, but in our day the most well-known version is that of Aristotle:

> Aristotle argued [in *Nicomachean Ethics* 1.7–8 (1097a15–99b8)] that happiness satisfies these conditions for the highest human good: (1) as ultimate end, it is most choiceworthy, that is, chosen always and only for itself and never for the sake of something else; (2) it is complete and comprehensive, including the virtues as intrinsic goods and external goods insofar as they insure (3) its self-sufficiency, namely, the inclusion of all things that are good for human beings, especially those over which we have control, for example, virtue; (4) it cannot be increased by the addition of any other good; and (5) it is most pleasant in itself.[1]

1. John Bussanich, s.v. "Happiness, Eudaimonism," in *Augustine through the Ages: An Encyclopedia*, ed. Allan D. Fitzgerald and John C. Cavadini (Grand Rapids, MI: William B. Eerdmans Publishing Co., 1999), 413–414. Simply stated, Aristotle took happiness to be the activity of the human soul in accordance with complete virtue over an entire lifetime (cf. *Nicomachean Ethics*, 1098a16–19). For an excellent treatment of Aristotle's eudaimonism and the tradition of "virtue ethics" that arose from it, see Alasdair C. MacIntyre, *After Virtue: A Study in Moral Theory* (Notre Dame: University of Notre Dame Press, 2007).

In order to better understand the distinctive character of Augustine's eudaimonism, we would do well to note a few general characteristics common to all eudaimonist theories, as well as a few specific characteristics that distinguish one such theory from another.

Generally, all eudaimonist theories have at least three common elements. First, unlike many modern theories of ethics and educational philosophy, eudaimonist accounts are unabashedly grounded in the conviction that human nature is both stable and knowable (neither in constant flux nor beyond our grasp as intellectual beings). By means of rational inquiry, we can come to know human nature not only as it currently *does* exist but also as it *could* exist in a state of perfection. Second, we can rationally discern how to get from where we currently are to where we aspire to be. This general approach to ethics and education proceeds from ends to principles to means. Having identified what the ultimate end of man is, the eudaimonist contends, we may proceed from first principles to the means of arriving at perfection. Lastly, the third common feature of eudaimonist accounts is that the practice of the virtues, or the moral and intellectual excellences of the human soul, is the central means by which we may approach perfection.

With the aforesaid similarities in mind, we also should note the kinds of differences that distinguish one eudaimonist account from another. First, there are differences in the understanding of what happiness consists of. Does it involve the body, the soul, or both? Is the happiness in question only what may be attained in this life, or is the happiness of our earthly existence but an imperfect foretaste of the full and perfect happiness found in the life hereafter? Second, there are significant differences from one eudaimonist theory to another regarding what the virtues are, how they are to be defined, and what, if any, order exists among them. Finally, there also are key differences regarding "where" we begin. In other words, what exactly is man's condition this side of perfection? What accounts for our current condition? Is our attempt to exercise moral and intellectual virtue enough? Apart from external aid, can man, through his own efforts, attain perfection? Augustine's account of happiness and his understanding of the ultimate purpose of education are best understood against this broad backdrop.

Happiness (*Beatitudo*) in *On the Happy Life*

From the time of the Cassiciacum dialogues, the earliest of Augustine's extant writings, Augustine makes an account of happiness, or "beatitude" (*beatitudo*), central to his philosophy of education, connecting the final end of human life to the ultimate goal of teaching and learning. Significantly, these four dialogues together dramatize what has been described as a "pedagogy in action":

> Through the *Contra Academicos* Augustine draws attention to the process of the discovery of truth; in the *De beata vita* we see unfolded the quest for the happy life; in the *De ordine* is uncovered the proper order of learning; through the *Soliloquia* we learn the right method for gaining knowledge of God and the soul.[2]

First, we will take a look at *De beata vita* (*On the Happy Life*) in order to see the beginnings of Augustine's account of happiness. From there, we will consider the Cassiciacum dialogues in general to see what they reveal about Augustine's early philosophy of education. Then we will discuss the development of Augustine's account of happiness in his later works. What we will find is a natural unfolding that shows how Augustine's concept of happiness and

2. Ryan N. S. Topping, *Happiness and Wisdom: Augustine's Early Theology of Education* (Washington, DC: The Catholic University of America Press, 2012), 71–72.

its attainment was progressively enriched through his ever-deeper understanding of his philosophical and theological sources.

> *Augustine makes an account of happiness, or "beatitude"* (beatitudo), *central to his philosophy of education, connecting the final end of human life to the ultimate goal of teaching and learning.*

Composed during the autumn of 386, *On the Happy Life* sheds light upon Augustine's early understanding of happiness. As he awaits baptism and reception into the Catholic Church, Augustine is already firmly convinced that the only way to be truly happy is to enjoy God. The entire philosophical quest for truth is ordered to this end.[3] After the interlocutors in the dialogue establish that everyone wants to be happy,[4] they begin to consider what constitutes happiness. While having what one wants is often considered essential for happiness, it is clearly not sufficient, as Augustine's mother, Monica, points out: "If [a man] wants and has good things, he is happy, but if he wants bad things, even if he has them, he is unhappy."[5] At this point, the interlocutors decide

---

3. See Michael Fiedrowicz and Roland Teske, SJ, "Introduction," in *Trilogy on Faith and Happiness* [Augustine's *The Happy Life, Faith in the Unseen, The Advantage of Believing*], trans. Roland Teske, SJ, Michael G. Campbell, OSA, and Ray Kearney, vol. 6 of *The Works of St. Augustine* (Hyde Park, NY: New City Press, 2010), 12:

> Like all ancient thinkers, Augustine was convinced that the desire for happiness . . . was universal. Like all Christian thinkers, he was convinced that happiness was ultimately attainable only in the enjoyment of God. The whole purpose of philosophizing was . . . the attainment of happiness, and the whole purpose of worshiping the true God was the attainment of the happy life, as Augustine insists again and again in *The City of God* [see, e.g., XIX, 1].

4. See Augustine, *The Happy Life*, in *Trilogy on Faith and Happiness*, 10. Unless otherwise indicated, all quotations of *The Happy Life* are from this edition.
5. Augustine, 10. In light of Monica's comments, compare Augustine's later remark in *The Trinity*, trans. Edmund Hill, OP, vol. 5 of *The Works of St. Augustine* (Hyde Park, NY: New City Press, 2012), 13.5.8: "Thus no one is happy but the man who has everything he wants, and wants nothing wrongly." Unless otherwise indicated, all quotations of *On the Trinity* are from this edition. Since the title of the English translation was shortened to *The Trinity*, we have attempted to avoid confusion by citing it in this book as follows: Augustine, *On the Trinity* (*The Trinity* trans.)

to consider "what we should want and what things we ought to desire" in order to be happy.[6] They quickly agree that whatever "it" is, it "has to be something that lasts forever and isn't dependent on good luck or subject to misfortune"; and soon thereafter they agree that "whoever has God is happy."[7] The conversation then turns to examine exactly who it is that "has God."[8] As Augustine leads the discussion, the interlocutors make headway in their pursuit of this question and those that follow from it. Eventually, on the third day of their conversation, the question under consideration is "What is wisdom?"[9] Responding to this question finally brings resolution to their earlier query regarding who "has God":

> What should we call wisdom if not that wisdom which is God's? We have it on the authority of God himself that the Son of God is God's wisdom, and the Son of God is surely God. . . . But what do you think wisdom is, if not truth? For Scripture also says, *I am the truth* (John 14:6). . . . Whoever shall have come to the highest limit through the truth is happy. For minds to have God is precisely this: To enjoy God. . . . That, then, is full satiety of minds, namely, the happy life, to know piously and perfectly that by which you are led into the truth, that truth which you enjoy, and that through which you are joined to the highest limit.[10]

There are three things we should note about these conclusions. First, we see that at this point in his reflections on the happy life, Augustine presents the "having" of God as the mind's attainment of wisdom, which in turn is truth. At first glance, this could sound like a fairly intellectualist account of happiness. The attainment of the happy life is described in terms of the "full satiety of minds." Second, however, we must also note that such knowledge, though

6. Augustine, *The Happy Life*, 10.
7. Augustine, 11.
8. Augustine, 12 ff.
9. Augustine, 33.
10. Augustine, 34–35.

presented as the satisfaction of the mind, is nevertheless a knowledge of and through a person, namely Jesus Christ, the Son of God. In some sense, the happy life is conceived as a union with God himself. Finally, we should attend to the fact that even in these early writings Augustine has a place for authority in his philosophical pursuit of the truth. The dialogue reaches its highest conclusion only by recourse to Sacred Scripture. As Augustine puts it, "We have it on the authority of God himself." Moreover, as the dialogue is advancing toward its conclusion, Augustine makes repeated reference (or allusion) to a "divine source" that enables him to discern the truth of what is said.[11] Beyond his reliance upon the authority of the Bible, there is a more fundamental reliance upon God himself teaching Augustine inwardly. We will return to the place of authority and especially to the doctrine of Christ as "Inner Teacher" in later chapters. For now, it is sufficient to note that from his earliest extant writings, Augustine is committed to *both* reason *and* authority—or, as medieval thinkers would later frame it, both faith and reason—as legitimate and indeed crucial sources of truth in the pursuit of wisdom.

Interlude: On Philosophy as a Way of Life in the Cassiciacum Dialogues

Before discussing the development of Augustine's understanding of happiness and the happy life in his later writings, we would do well to get a fuller sense of what the Cassiciacum dialogues in general teach us about Augustine's early philosophy of education. Recall from the second chapter the two distinct schools of thought

11. See, for example, his response to the quotation from Cicero's *Hortensius* in section 10. See also Augustine, *Against the Academicians and the Teacher* (Indianapolis: Hackett Publishing Co., 1995), 3.5.11, where he contends that only some "divine spirit" can show man what the truth is.

in the West on the nature and purpose of education: the Orators and the Philosophers—that is, the rhetorical tradition and the philosophical tradition. To be sure, we find in these dialogues the influence of the rhetorical tradition in which Augustine was trained as a young man. With the exception of Monica and Augustine's cousins, Lartidianus and Rusticus, all those present at Cassiciacum had received a traditional Roman education in grammar, including training in the reading of classic literary texts such as the works of Virgil and Cicero. The dramatic action of these dialogues is in important ways informed by the texts and pedagogical methods of the rhetorical tradition. In *Contra Academicos* (*Against the Academic Skeptics*), for example, the interlocutors take nearly seven days off to read and discuss certain books of Virgil's *Aeneid*. In serving as the leader of these discussions, it may be that Augustine intends to depict himself in the role of a Roman *grammaticus*, a teacher whose duties included commenting on classical texts. Moreover, some scholars see in Augustine's long speech against Cicero in *Against the Academic Skeptics* (3.16.35–17.37) a model declamation delivered by an orator. Even granting all this, however, the education that Augustine conducted at Cassiciacum was more one of a school of philosophy than one of a school of rhetoric.

Like any good philosopher, Augustine begins by dispelling the doubts of skepticism and engendering confidence in his companions that the truth can be known. For Augustine, the philosophical life begins with an act of hope.

First and most obviously, Augustine chose to present these works as *dialogues*, the literary form most closely associated with Plato and the subsequent philosophical tradition. More importantly, in these works the literary form is no mere "window dressing" but a poetic presentation of Augustine's commitment to dialectic as the principal means of pursuing the truth. This fact becomes clearer when we reflect upon the structure and content of the Cassiciacum dialogues taken as a literary and philosophical whole. In the first dialogue, *Against the Academic Skeptics*, Augustine and his friends establish truth as the worthy and attainable goal of the philosophical way of life. Like any good philosopher, Augustine begins by dispelling the doubts of skepticism and engendering confidence in his companions that the truth can be known. For Augustine, the philosophical life begins with an act of hope.[12] Then, following in the footsteps of Cicero (in his *Hortensius*), Augustine composes his own exhortation to the life of philosophy in *On the Happy Life*. Once happiness has been firmly established as the destination of the journey, Augustine proceeds in *De ordine* (*On Order*) to unfold the proper order of learning—that is, the road map that will lead Augustine and his companions to their journey's end.[13] Finally, in *Soliloquies*, a term coined by Augustine himself, he engages in a "dialogic monologue"[14] between himself and "Reason" in order to demonstrate the correct method of acquiring knowledge of God and the soul.[15] Taken together, these four dialogues embody Augustine's early understanding of the nature of education in

12. Speaking of *Against the Academic Skeptics* in his *Revisions*, Augustine tells us his intention in writing the work: "My purpose was to drive from my mind with as many reasons as I could those arguments of theirs that cause many to despair of finding anything true and that prevent the wise person from assenting to anything and from accepting anything at all as clear and certain, since to them everything appears obscure and uncertain" (Augustine, *Revisions*, trans. Boniface Ramsey, vol. 2 of *The Works of St. Augustine* [Hyde Park, NY: New City Press, 2010], 1.1). Unless otherwise indicated, all quotations of *Revisions* are from this edition.

13. We will discuss this road map in the next chapter when we examine the place of the liberal arts in Augustine's theory and practice of education.

14. Joanne McWilliam, s.v. "*Soliloquia*," in *Augustine through the Ages*, 806–807.

15. Thus the Cassiciacum dialogues are "dialogical" in different senses. The first three mentioned above enact a dialogue among persons committed to pursuing the truth. The fourth and final work portrays "inner dialogue" as a means of gaining self-knowledge precisely *through* knowledge of God. Augustine prays at the beginning of the second book of *Soliloquies*, "O God . . . may I know myself, may I know You" (my translation: *noverim me, noverim te*). On the genre of soliloquy and its development in late antiquity, see Brian Stock's *Augustine's Inner Dialogue: Philosophical Soliloquy in Late Antiquity* (New York: Cambridge University Press, 2010). We will return to the notion of inner dialogue and its relation to self-knowledge in later chapters.

theory as well as in practice. "In terms of manner," Topping contends, "Augustine's Cassiciacum dialogues present a living model for education. As Hadot has argued, ancient philosophy did not only concern itself with theory. Schools also represented an alternative and superior way of life: practical and intellectual disciplines were cultivated with this aim in sight."[16]

Augustine carries out his philosophical inquiry in the acknowledged presence of God, regularly imploring God's assistance and thus making prayer an integral part of the philosophical *pursuit of truth.*

While Augustine is clearly and deeply indebted to the philosophical tradition, the "way of life" that he champions is in certain significant respects quite different from earlier philosophies. First, as has been pointed out already, Augustine affords an enduring and central place to authority in his pursuit of truth. This difference sets Augustine's theory and practice of education apart from that of all his predecessors. A second difference, closely related to the first, is that while dialectic is the principal mode of inquiry and reason is given relatively free rein in these dialogues, such rational dialectic—insofar as it adequately attains the truth—could never in principle contradict the authority of either Christ, the Incarnate Word, or the Bible, the Word of God revealed to mankind. A pioneer of the integration of faith and reason, Augustine is confident that a proper understanding of the revealed truths of Christianity and the results of philosophical inquiry properly conducted can never ultimately be in conflict. Finally, Augustine carries out his philosophical inquiry in the acknowledged presence of God, regularly imploring God's assistance and thus making prayer an integral part of the *philosophical* pursuit of truth.

---

16. Topping, *Happiness and Wisdom*, 71. In this quotation, Topping refers to Pierre Hadot's seminal work, *Philosophy as a Way of Life: Spiritual Exercises from Socrates to Foucault*, trans. Michael Chase, ed. Arnold I. Davidson (Malden, MA: Blackwell Publishing, 1995).

As mentioned earlier, for Augustine there is no philosophy of education without a theology of education. At the very end of *On the Happy Life*, Monica offers a brief prayer to the Trinity and then sums up their findings: "This is without doubt the happy life, and that life is perfect toward which we can, we must presume, be quickly brought through solid faith, lively hope, and burning love."[17] Significantly, it is through the theological virtues, which are excellences of the soul infused by God as gifts, that we are brought to perfect happiness. Augustine concurs with Monica, offering a prayer of thanks to "the highest and true God, the Father, to the Lord, the deliverer of souls."[18]

Happiness in Augustine's Later Writings

Turning to the broader question of happiness in the writings Augustine composed after the Cassiciacum dialogues, we will focus primarily on three works. Augustine began the first of these, *De libero arbitrio voluntatis* (*On Free Choice of the Will*), in Rome shortly after his conversion, writing the first "book" (or part) in 387–388. He wrote the second and third books in Hippo after his ordination to the priesthood in 391. Along with confirming the aforementioned positions that the one who "has God" is happy[19] and that happiness is attained through wisdom, which is understood in terms of truth,[20] *On Free Choice of the Will* also clearly and succinctly unites goodness, desirability, and pleasure: "Happy is he who enjoys the highest good."[21]

17. Augustine, *The Happy Life*, 35.

18. Augustine, 36.

19. See Augustine, *On Free Choice of the Will*, trans. Thomas Williams (Indianapolis: Hackett Publishing Company, 1993), 2.16.

20. Augustine, 2.13.

21. Augustine, 2.13. These observations and this translation are Bussanich's, s.v. "Happiness, Eudaimonism," in *Augustine through the Ages*, 413.

In *Confessions*, which he wrote between 397 and 401, Augustine gives an extended meditation on the nature of happiness (chapters 20–23 of book X), which begins as follows: "How then am I to seek you, Lord? When I seek you, my God, what I am seeking is a life of happiness. Let me seek you that my soul may live, for as my body draws its life from my soul, so does my soul draw its life from you."[22] Here Augustine emphasizes that God is the very life of the soul. When we discuss *On the Trinity* in a subsequent chapter, we will see a more fully developed account of what this means for Augustine.

A second crucial contribution of *Confessions* is a more explicit statement of happiness as rejoicing in the truth. First, Augustine presents the happy life as rejoicing in God: "A joy there is that is not granted to the godless, but to those only who worship you without looking for reward, because you yourself are their joy. This is the happy life, and this alone: to rejoice in you, about you, and because of you."[23] In the next chapter, Augustine modifies his account as follows: "Now the happy life is joy in the truth; and that means joy in you, who are the Truth [John 14:6], O God who shed the light of salvation on my face, my God."[24] This account of happiness from book X of *Confessions* confirms Augustine's understanding as found in both *On the Happy Life* and *On Free Choice of the Will* and establishes "rejoicing in the truth" as his basic definition of happiness.

Finally, in *De civitate Dei* (*City of God*), composed between 413 and 427, Augustine gives a comprehensive treatment of salvation history. He frames his account in terms of two "cities," the City of God and the Earthly City, which are defined by the objects of their love: "The earthly city was created by self-love reaching the point of

22. Augustine, *The Confessions*, 10.20.29.

23. Augustine, 10.22.32.

24. Augustine, 10.23.33. Compare 1 Corinthians 13:6: "Love does not delight in (χαίρει) unrighteousness, but rejoices in (συγχαίρει) the truth" (my translation).

contempt for God, the [City of God] by the love of God carried as far as contempt of self."[25] Building upon the notion of rest and peace as the attainment of worthy objects of desire, a notion developed in detail in his *Confessions*, in *City of God* Augustine characterizes the happiness of the blessed as follows: "We see, then, that the Supreme Good of the City of God is everlasting and perfect peace, which is not the peace through which men pass in their mortality, in their journey from birth to death, but that peace in which they remain in their immortal state, experiencing no adversity at all."[26] Although in his earlier works Augustine speaks as if one could be perfectly happy in this mortal life, his mature works firmly deny this possibility. In *On the Trinity*, for example, Augustine contends, "Only when a man who is faithful and good in these unhappy conditions passes from this life to the happy life, will there really and truly be what now cannot possibly be, namely that a man lives as he would."[27] Similarly, in *City of God* he says, "As . . . we are saved in hope, it is in hope that we have been made happy; and as we do not yet possess a present salvation, but await salvation in the future, so we do not enjoy a present happiness, but look forward to happiness in the future, as we look forward 'with steadfast endurance' [cf. Romans 8:24-25]."[28] Lastly, in the *City of God* we also see Augustine's insistence that the mediation of Christ is essential to happiness: "[I]t was necessary that the mediator between God and man should have a transient mortality, and a permanent blessedness [*beatitudo*], so that through that which is transient he might be conformed to the condition of those who are doomed to die, and might bring them back from the dead to that which is permanent."[29]

---

25. Augustine, *City of God*, trans. Henry Bettenson, Penguin Classics (New York: Penguin Books, 2003), 14.28. Unless otherwise indicated, all quotations of *City of God* are from this edition.
26. Augustine, 19.20.
27. Augustine, *On the Trinity* (*The Trinity* trans.), 13.7.10.
28. Augustine, *City of God*, 19.4.
29. Augustine, 9.15. Indeed, the burden of this entire chapter is to establish Christ as the mediator between God and men, and thus the only way to return to happiness in God's presence.

RECAPITULATION

In this chapter on the nature and purpose of education, we have moved freely through Augustine's writings, starting with *On the Happy Life*, then broadening our focus to consider all of the Cassiciacum dialogues, and finally noting what a few later writings contribute to the question. Given the far-reaching nature of this inquiry, perhaps it is helpful to conclude by drawing together the various strands to give a brief synopsis of our findings. First, for Augustine the purpose of education is to help us attain happiness, which is rejoicing in the truth. This truth is God himself, who is also Wisdom. The perfect happiness we seek is not attainable in this mortal life; instead, as we are saved in hope, so also we look forward in hope to perfect happiness. Not everything we want will lead us toward happiness; thus, part of a proper education is learning "what we should want and what things we ought to desire." To be sure, happiness involves the "full satiety of the mind," but this is within the context of enjoying God, of somehow being united to him.

Although Augustine is certainly indebted to the rhetorical tradition for his educational philosophy and pedagogy, he is even more indebted to the philosophical tradition. Nevertheless, the "way of life" that Augustine advocates is distinctive, relying not only on the authority of Sacred Scripture[30] but also on the witness of an inner "divine source" to help one discern the truth. The highest reaches of happiness are simply not attainable without divine assistance, and even the highest virtues—faith, hope, and love—are themselves gifts from God and not attainable by dint of human effort. While grounded in the deep and rich rhetorical and

30. For Augustine, of course, God's authority is not restricted to Sacred Scripture alone. As Michael Foley rightly notes, Augustine "consistently speaks of the 'mysteries' of the faith, which are disclosed not only through Scripture but through liturgy and other sources. See *Against the [Academic Skeptics]* 2.1.1; *On the Happy Life* 1.4; and *On Order* 2.5.15, 2.6.16, 2.9.27, 2.17.46" (correspondence with author).

philosophical traditions of Greco-Roman antiquity, Augustine's own distinctive philosophy of education is even more deeply rooted in the Judeo-Christian tradition.

Chapter Four
"Arts Reputed 'Liberal'": On Liberal Education and Happiness

In the last chapter, we focused on the ultimate end of education. We turn now to an account of Augustine's understanding of the traditional "beginnings" of education: the liberal arts. Later in the Western tradition, these arts came to be known as the *trivium* (three ways)—grammar, dialectic (logic), and rhetoric—and the *quadrivium* (four ways)—arithmetic, geometry, music, and astronomy. In his early writings, Augustine sees the liberal arts as able to lead the student from contemplation of the created order to the contemplation of God as the eternal and immutable Cause of all created things.[1] Later on, however, Augustine comes to have a more measured assessment of their potential to "liberate" those who are trained in them. In light of this development in Augustine's thought on the matter, this chapter has two parts. In the first, we will explore another of Augustine's Cassiciacum dialogues, *De ordine* (*On Order*), in which Augustine lays out a formidable defense of the liberal arts and their foundational role in a liberal education. In the second part, we will see what Augustine has to say about (and to do with) the liberal arts in his later writings, especially in *Revisions* and *Confessions*.

1. See, e.g., *De ordine, De musica, Retractationes.*

On Order: The First Christian Account of the Liberal Arts

Although other Christian authors made mention and use of the liberal arts before him, Augustine's *On Order* is the earliest extant Christian account that offers a systematic treatment of the liberal arts and their proper place in liberal education. To call an education "liberal" is simply to claim that, in one or more ways, the education "frees" the one who is trained in it. By Augustine's time, the liberal arts had long been conceived as the best starting point for such an education for freedom.[2]

In the opening lines of *On Order*, Augustine underscores the importance and difficulty of discerning order: "To grasp and retain the order proper to each and every thing, and then indeed to see or explain the order of the whole by which this world is held together and ruled . . . is extremely rare and difficult for men to do."[3] The emphasis is clearly upon understanding the parts in terms of the whole. Augustine offers an example to clarify:

> [I]f someone could see so little that in viewing a mosaic his eye could take in no more than the span of one little cube, he would criticize the artisan as ignorant of order and composition. And he would

---

2. This is not to say, of course, that previous authors necessarily called them the "liberal arts," or that there was universal agreement on what arts were to be included in the list. Even so, there is abundant evidence from Greek and Roman authors—Plato, Aristotle, Cicero, Seneca, et al.—that some such arts were considered the proper beginning of a liberal education.

3. Augustine, *On Order*, in "The Cassiciacum Dialogues of St. Augustine," trans. Michael P. Foley (unpublished manuscript, 2011), 1.1.1. Unless otherwise indicated, all quotations of *On Order* are from Foley's translation. Later in the work, the interlocutors offer two accounts of order. According to the first, order is "that which, if we keep it in this life, will lead us to God, and which, unless we keep it in this life, we won't come to God" (1.9.27). According to the latter account, "Order is that through which all things that God has ordained are guided" (1.10.28). Neither of these is a formal definition. When discussing the "peace of the whole universe" in *City of God*, Augustine offers something closer to a definition: "Order is the arrangement of things equal and unequal [or 'similar and dissimilar'] in a pattern which assigns to each its proper position" (19.13).

> have the impression that the assortment of little stones was in disarray from the fact that those inlaid pieces, harmonizing into the splendor of a single beauty, could not be seen and surveyed all at once. The same thing happens with less educated men who are not able to comprehend and consider with their feeble minds the harmony and co-fittingness of the whole.[4]

Like Plato before him, Augustine considers education as a means of perfecting one's intellectual vision (the "mind's eye"), sharpening one's judgment, and bringing about a rightly ordered soul by gaining a rightly ordered knowledge of things. Again like Plato, Augustine sees the liberal arts as crucial to this process.[5] Furthermore, Augustine presents training in the liberal arts as a means of healing the soul:

> The greatest cause of this error [i.e., the one described above] is that man is unknown to himself. Yet in order for someone to come to know himself, he needs the great habit of withdrawing from the senses and of collecting his soul into itself and holding itself there. Those who reach such a stage . . . either singe by solitude or heal by the liberal disciplines certain wounds of opinion which the course of daily life inflicts.[6]

When the soul returns to itself, "it understands what is the beauty of the whole [*universitas*], which in fact comes from the word 'one' [*unum*]."[7]

4. Augustine, *On Order*, 1.1.2.

5. See, for example, the discussion of the mathematical "plan of studies" in book VII of Plato's *Republic*.

6. Augustine, *On Order*, 1.2.3.

7. Augustine, 1.2.3.

Like Plato before him, Augustine considers education as a means of perfecting one's intellectual vision (the "mind's eye"), sharpening one's judgment, and bringing about a rightly ordered soul by gaining a rightly ordered knowledge of things. Again like Plato, Augustine sees the liberal arts as crucial to this process.

How exactly do the liberal arts help in this process? Augustine presents an example from geometry:

> For example, regardless of how large a circle is, it has only one midpoint . . . at which all lines converge; and although the parts of an entire circumference can be divided an infinite number of times, there is still nothing else except that one midpoint by which all other parts are evenly measured and which rules over all, so to speak, by a kind of law of equality.[8]

Notice how this fundamental truth of geometry—that a circle is "measured" and "ruled" by its center—becomes an occasion for philosophical reflection on the question of unity and plurality. The one "midpoint" is a principle of the circle as a whole; the circle first becomes intelligible *qua circle* by attending to its center.[9] In like manner, the liberal arts place before us the principles, or "first things," that enable us to make a good beginning in our knowledge of various disciplines. As such, practicing the liberal arts involves an inquiry into the causes proper to certain fields of study.[10]

---

8. Augustine, 1.2.3.
9. Compare Euclid's definition of a circle: "A circle is a plane figure contained by one line such that *all the straight lines falling upon it from one point* among those lying within the figure equal one another" (*Elements*, Book I, Definition 15 [emphasis added]).
10. In the drama of the dialogue, Augustine humorously introduces the theme of seeking after causes when the interlocutors are awakened by the sound of running water and offer different accounts of the cause. They eventually decide it is leaves caught in the plumbing system, and then move on to more exalted questions, such as whence wonder arises.

Significantly, Augustine connects an education grounded in the liberal arts with love, desire, and the happy life:

> [A]n education in the liberal disciplines (if, of course, moderate and concise), produces lovers more lively, more persevering, and better groomed for embracing the truth; and as a result they more ardently desire, more consistently pursue, and finally, more sweetly cling to that which is called . . . the happy life.[11]

Augustine connects an education grounded in the liberal arts with love, desire, and the happy life.

What remarkable claims![12] For Augustine, training in the liberal arts is not simply (or even principally) a matter of conveying information from teacher to student. Instead it is an introduction to a philosophical way of life, an introduction that not only forms the mind but also engenders love for the truth and instills a deep desire to pursue and embrace the happy life.

In the second book, Augustine comments on the way in which a study of the mathematical arts can lead to philosophy and ultimately to God himself:

> Now in music, in geometry, in the movements of the stars [astronomy], in the laws of numbers [arithmetic], order so dominates that if one longs to see its fount, its actual inner sanctuary, so to speak, one must either discover it in these [disciplines] or be led through them to it without any error. For an education such as this, if one uses it moderately, . . . rears a soldier or even a general for philosophy, so that wherever

11. Augustine, *On Order*, 1.8.24.

12. To be sure, the claims are remarkable; but as anyone who has led students through works such as Aristotle's *Categories*, Euclid's *Elements*, or Ptolemy's *Almagest* can attest, these are indeed the results of a serious training in the liberal arts.

> he wants to he flies up to and reaches that Supreme Measure [i.e., God] beyond which he is neither able to, nor should he, nor does he, desire to ask for anything; and he leads the many to It as well.[13]

Furthermore, Augustine contends that observing this proper order and measure in the study of the liberal arts is crucial. In both of the last two quotations, Augustine warns against an immoderate pursuit of these liberal disciplines. This naturally leads to the question: "What would it mean to pursue such education immoderately?" After all, isn't knowledge inherently good? And if so, isn't acquiring more knowledge simply better than acquiring less? A little further on, Augustine explains the problem, reasoning: "If one dares to rush into knowing these things blindly and without the order of the disciplines, he will become curious instead of studious, credulous instead of learned, incredulous instead of cautious."[14] For Augustine, curiosity is a vice of excess opposed to the virtue of studiosity. Whereas the studious person will keep the proper measure and order in study, the curious person will flit from one thing to another, observing no order and measure in his insatiable pursuit of knowledge.[15] In addition, pursuing knowledge without order and measure also will lead to either credulity or incredulity, the vice of excess or defect, with respect to belief. Clearly, for Augustine, intellectual formation and moral formation go hand in hand.

In the second book, Augustine also gives an account of each of the liberal arts: first grammar, dialectic, and rhetoric; then music,

---

13. Augustine, *On Order*, 2.5.14.

14. Augustine, 2.5.17.

15. The way that many "surf" the Internet today is a perfect illustration of the vice Augustine is describing here. With no clear end in view and no sense of proportion in the pursuit, one can easily spend countless hours clicking from one link to another, "informing" oneself without really learning anything of lasting importance. As Michael Foley rightly observes, the curiosity Augustine censures is "a disordered intellectual itch that is keen to acquire useless or trivial information such as gossip or grotesque sights or that has an appetite for laudable knowledge but in a perverse or inordinate manner" (Foley, "The Cassiciacum Dialogues of St. Augustine," 175).

geometry, astronomy, and arithmetic (or "number").[16] The liberal arts are learned "partly for their usefulness in living, partly for the knowledge and contemplation of things."[17] Among the liberal arts, dialectic has, for Augustine, pride of place. Dialectic "teaches teaching, it teaches learning: in it, reason itself shows itself and reveals what it is, what it wants, what it can do. It knows how to know; it alone not only wants to produce knowers, but it also can."[18] In essence, then, dialectic is understood by Augustine to be the science of knowledge as such and helps us to understand what it means to know the objects of any and every discipline. This being the case, dialectic is fundamental to our ability to order all of our knowledge and thus to make sense of the whole.

Among the liberal arts, dialectic has, for Augustine, pride of place. Dialectic "teaches teaching, it teaches learning: in it, reason itself shows itself and reveals what it is, what it wants, what it can do. It knows how to know; it alone not only wants to produce knowers, but it also can."

In summary, then, Augustine presents the liberal arts as the beginning points of a liberal education, by their nature propaedeutic to other, higher studies. They are tools by means of which we can discern the order of the created universe. Like tiles in a mosaic, they each have their own value, but they are most intelligible—and shed most light on the intelligibility of other things—when considered as parts of a larger whole. They enable

16. See Augustine, *On Order*, 2.12.35–2.15.43.

17. Augustine, 2.16.44.

18. Augustine, 2.13.38. For these reasons, dialectic (or logic as traditionally understood) came to be known as both the "art of arts" and the "rational science." (See, for example, the commentaries of St. Thomas Aquinas on Aristotle's *De Interpretatione* and *Posterior Analytics*.)

those trained in them to ascend to higher studies: first philosophy, and ultimately theology.[19]

The Liberal Arts Reconsidered

Late in his life (428), Augustine reviewed all of his published works in order, summarizing and commenting on them in *Retractationes* (*Revisions*). In a prologue to this work, Augustine identifies his central task: "to reconsider my works from an uncompromisingly critical perspective, whether they be books or letters or sermons, and in these pages to single out for censure what I disapprove of."[20] While many of his works are merely summarized and escape self-censure, the Cassiciacum dialogues are not as fortunate. Beyond occasional factual errors in the dialogues, Augustine is most concerned with his overconfident statements about the possibility of attaining happiness in this mortal life as well as man's ability, through his own effort, to ascend to the contemplation of the highest things. Speaking of *On Order* in particular, he seeks to qualify his enthusiasm about the liberal arts: "I attributed a great deal to the liberal disciplines, which many holy persons know very little about (while several of those who do know something about them are not holy)."[21]

Regarding Augustine's reconsideration of the liberal arts later in life, scholars are divided.[22] To what extent does Augustine's view

19. The ascent here is envisioned as both *conceptual* and *curricular*. In other words, there is a natural conceptual progression from the liberal arts to philosophy and theology. But this conceptual progression may be—indeed, *should be*—reflected in a curricular progression as well, given the nature of reality and of man's capacity to know.

20. Augustine, *Revisions*, Prologue.1.

21. Augustine, 3.2.

22. For a sampling of different perspectives on this question, see Karla Pollman and Mark Vessey, eds., *Augustine and the Disciplines: From Cassiciacum to* Confessions (New York: Oxford University Press, 2005); and Kim Paffenroth and Kevin L. Hughes, eds., *Augustine and Liberal Education* (New York: Lexington Books, 2008).

of the liberal arts really change? His comments here in *Revisions* do qualify his account in *On Order*, but they hardly amount to a repudiation of his earlier position. Indeed, one could argue that they simply make explicit something already present implicitly in the drama of the Cassiciacum dialogues. As mentioned above, his mother is typically present for the conversations. While Monica lacks the training in the liberal arts that many of the other interlocutors enjoy, she nevertheless is presented as correcting the mistakes of her liberally educated partners in dialogue. Her comments are regularly insightful and at times decisive, effectively settling the matter in question. Although untutored in the liberal arts, she manifests a wisdom that derives from her piety and her reliance on the authority of Sacred Scripture and the teachings of the Catholic Church. Clearly, then, at the time of his writing *On Order* and the other Cassiciacum dialogues, Augustine was aware that one may be holy without a knowledge of the liberal arts. We also can safely assume that Augustine already knew that one may have a knowledge of the liberal arts and yet fail to be holy, given what he says in *Confessions* about his own teachers of grammar and rhetoric as a young man.[23]

To deepen our understanding of Augustine's mature position on the liberal arts, let us turn now to *Confessions*. Here Augustine makes several comments that make it seem as though his views on the liberal arts in general, and on the art of rhetoric in particular, have substantially changed. Describing his years of Manichean wandering, Augustine recounts in book IV how "[he] and others like [him] were seduced and seducers, deceived [themselves] and deceivers of others amid a welter of desires: publicly through the arts reputed 'liberal,' and secretly under the false name of religion."[24] Near the end of the same book, Augustine poses the rhetorical question:

23. We will discuss Augustine's teachers and their influence in greater detail in the next chapter. For now, suffice it to say that many of them were not exemplars of holiness.

24. Augustine, *Confessions*, 4.1.1.

> What profit was it to me that I, rascally slave of selfish ambitions that I was, read and understood by myself as many books as I could get concerning the so-called liberal arts? . . . I had turned my back to the light and my face to the things it illuminated, and so no light played upon my face, or on the eyes that perceived them.[25]

Regarding Augustine's position on rhetoric in particular, critical comments abound. Perhaps most pointed are his remarks in book IX where he describes his decision to renounce his career as a professor of rhetoric: "I believed it to be pleasing in your [God's] sight that I should withdraw the service of my tongue from the market of speechifying."[26] He even goes so far as to call his former position "a professorial chair of lying."[27]

On the other hand, Augustine also makes several comments in *Confessions* that seem to imply he has retained a relatively high view of the liberal arts. First, he mentions his anticipation in hearing that Faustus, a Manichean bishop who many assured Augustine would answer his questions regarding astronomy, was reputed to be "particularly learned in the liberal arts."[28] As recounted earlier in chapter 1, when Faustus arrived, Augustine was deeply disappointed to discover Faustus was actually "a man ill-educated in the liberal arts."[29] Granted, one could argue that this apparently high estimation of the liberal arts was but a symptom of Augustine's depraved condition at the time. However, this is unlikely for a variety of reasons, and such an argument certainly does not apply in the case of another figure, Victorinus, a man who was clearly a model for Augustine and whom Augustine describes in *Confessions* as said to be "thoroughly conversant with

25. Augustine, 4.16.30.
26. Augustine, 9.2.2.
27. Augustine, 9.2.4.
28. Augustine, 5.3.3.
29. Augustine, 5.6.11.

all the liberal arts."[30] Victorinus's conversion to Christianity is in fact presented as a formative influence on Augustine's decision to follow in his footsteps.

Furthermore, in describing his ascent to God through memory in book X, Augustine dedicates several chapters to what he has learned through his study of the liberal arts,[31] and later presents the knowledge he has gained through the liberal arts as a crucial step in his intellectual ascent to God through memory. Finally, while he may have difficult things to say about the way rhetoric was customarily practiced in his day, Augustine's writing of *Confessions* itself betrays a very high view of the art. Scholars are in unanimous agreement that *Confessions* is nothing less than a rhetorical masterpiece.

Where does this leave us? The answer is that even in his mature works, Augustine has not abandoned the liberal arts. Instead, in his later years he simply takes great pains to argue that they are neither *necessary* for the ascent to God nor inherently *sufficient* for such an ascent, especially if divorced from their proper purpose within a liberal education ordered to truth and wisdom. We need to bear in mind that in his later years, Augustine is writing as a bishop of the Catholic Church. His enduring concern for excellent teaching is only heightened when he takes on his ecclesial duties, one of which is teaching the truth in charity to his Christian flock.

---

30. See Augustine, 8.2.3.

31. See Augustine, 10.9.16 ff.

CHAPTER FIVE

Augustine the Teacher: *Confessions*, *City of God*, *On the Trinity*, and *On Christian Teaching*

> Beloved, let us love one another; for love is of God,
> and he who loves is born of God and knows God.
> He who does not love does not know God; for God is love.
> In this the love of God was made manifest among us,
> that God sent his only Son into the world,
> so that we might live through him.
>
> —1 John 4:7-9 (RSV)

In this chapter we will explore four of Augustine's most influential works: *Confessions*, *City of God*, *On the Trinity*, and *On Christian Teaching*. Our purpose will be to see how the theory and practice of education laid out in the previous chapters are on display in Augustine's writing as a master teacher. Although we will consider many themes, the master theme will be Augustine's teaching on love. Of all the themes in his works, the nature of human love and our proper response to God's love are matters of utmost concern for Augustine as a teacher. Before considering these works, then, we need a general account of the significance and centrality of love in Augustine's philosophy and theology of education.[1]

---

1. In the following section on love in Augustine's writings, I rely heavily upon the excellent treatment of the topic found in Tarsicius J. van Bavel, OSA., s.v. "Love," in *Augustine through the Ages*, 509–516. I gratefully acknowledge my debt to this author, especially for his abundant references to love throughout Augustine's corpus. For other helpful overviews of love in St. Augustine's writings, see: (1) Hugh Feiss's "General Introduction" in *On Love: A Selection of Works of Hugh, Adam, Achard, Richard, and Godfrey of St. Victor*, ed. Hugh Feiss, OSB, vol. 2 of *Victorine Texts in Translation: Exegesis, Theology and Spirituality from the Abbey of St. Victor* (Hyde Park, NY: New City Press, 2012), 51–61; and (2) Etienne Gilson, *The Christian Philosophy of Saint Augustine*, trans. L. E. M. Lynch (New York: Random House, 1960), 165–169.

Love: Master Theme of a Master Teacher

In order to get our bearings, let us begin with a basic account of Augustine's understanding of love. In his writings, Augustine does not make a hard and fast distinction when he uses three Latin words for love: *amor*, *caritas*, and *dilectio*.[2] In a given context, any of these terms can refer to something praiseworthy or blameworthy, depending upon the object that is loved as well as upon the disposition of the one who loves. To provide a working definition of love, Tarsicius J. van Bavel draws together an account inspired by various texts of Augustine: "Love as such is an inclination, a movement, or a striving. . . . Love is the force of the soul and the life. We live on the basis of our love, and love determines life in a good or evil way."[3] In *On Order*, Augustine describes love as "the will to become one with the object which it loves; and, when it reaches its object, becomes one with it."[4] And in *On the Trinity*, he rhetorically asks, "And what is love but a kind of life coupling or trying to couple together two things, namely lover and what is being loved?"[5]

Love is central to Augustine's theology. Strikingly, in his seventh homily on the First Epistle of John, while commenting on 1 John 4:8 ("God is love"), Augustine boldly claims:

> What more could be said, brothers? If nothing were said in praise of love in all the pages of this epistle, if nothing at all were said in the other pages of the [S]criptures, and this were the one and only thing that we heard from the voice of the Spirit of

2. See Augustine, *City of God*, 14.7, where Augustine shows that Sacred Scripture itself does not make a clear-cut distinction in the use of these terms.

3. Van Bavel, "Love," 509.

4. Augustine, *On Order*, 2.18.48. This translation is van Bavel's.

5. Augustine, *On the Trinity* (*The Trinity* trans.), 8.10.14.

> God, that *God is love*, we wouldn't have to look for anything else.[6]

Most fundamentally, our love is a movement toward what we perceive to be good for us. Since God is in fact our ultimate good (*summum bonum*), the love of God is not only essential to human happiness; it *is* our happiness. For Augustine, we are distinguished by the character of our loves. What we love indicates what we are:

> Love alone . . . distinguishes between the children of God and the children of the devil. All may sign themselves with the sign of Christ's cross; all may respond "Amen"; all may sing "Alleluia"; all may be baptized; all may go into the churches; all may construct the walls of basilicas. The children of God aren't distinguished from the children of the devil except by charity.[7]

*Most fundamentally, our love is a movement toward what we perceive to be good for us. Since God is in fact our ultimate good (*summum bonum*), the love of God is not only essential to human happiness; it* is *our happiness.*

With the foregoing account of love in mind, it should not be surprising that for Augustine every virtue is a form of love. In his treatise *On the Morals of the Catholic Church and the Manichees*, Augustine says, "As to virtue leading us to the happy life, I hold virtue to be nothing else than [the] perfect love of God."

6. Augustine, *Homilies on the First Epistle of John*, trans. Boniface Ramsey, vol. 14 of *The Works of St. Augustine* (Hyde Park, NY: New City Press, 2008), 7.4. Unless otherwise indicated, all quotations of *Homilies on the First Epistle of John* are from this edition.

7. Augustine, 5.7.

Significantly, he presents the four classical cardinal (or "hinge") virtues as various forms of love:[8]

> For the fourfold division of virtue I regard as taken from four forms of love . . . I should have no hesitation in defining them: that temperance is love giving itself entirely to that which is loved; fortitude is the lover readily bearing all things for the sake of the loved object; justice is love serving only the loved object, and therefore ruling rightly; prudence is love distinguishing with sagacity between what hinders it and what helps it.[9]

Thus, the entire pursuit of moral and intellectual virtue in our attempt to attain happiness is conceived by Augustine as growth in love. Furthermore, from beginning to end, both education and happiness are matters of love. We are first taught love by God through the Incarnation,[10] and all the commandments of God are ordered toward love as their *telos*, or ultimate goal. In light of Augustine's comments on 1 Timothy 1:5 ("Love is the end of the commandment"), van Bavel explains:

> [For Augustine] love is the perfection to which all other precepts must be referred. It is the deepest meaning of all other prohibitions and commandments. . . . The reason for the incarnation of the Son of God is the revelation of God's love for the human being. Without the motive of teaching how much God loves us, and that we may learn to love him and our neighbors, there would be no reason why Jesus should have become our neighbor. . . . From this principle Augustine draws the conclusion: "Anyone who does not possess love, denies Christ's incarnation" (*ep. Jo.* 6.13–7.2).[11]

8. Augustine, *On the Morals of the Catholic Church and the Manichees*, 1.15.25. This and the following translation are from Topping, *St. Augustine*, 42.

9. Augustine, 1.15.25.

10. See Augustine's *De catechizandis rudibus* (*On the Instruction of Beginners*), 4.7–8, and *Homilies on the First Epistle of John*, 10.5.

11. Van Bavel, "Love," 510.

As we will see in what follows, the Incarnation is central to Augustine's understanding of love, and thus to his understanding of happiness. Through the Incarnation, God teaches us many things, but humility and love are foremost among them. In the end, those trained in love and incorporated into the Body of Christ will be sons of God:

> Which sons of God? The members of the Son of God [Christ]. And he himself also becomes a member by loving, and through love he comes to be in the structure of Christ's body, and there shall be one Christ loving himself. For, when the members love each other, the body loves itself.[12]

To love members of the Body of Christ is to love the Son of God and the Father as well.[13]

The Incarnation is central to Augustine's understanding of love, and thus to his understanding of happiness. Through the Incarnation, God teaches us many things, but humility and love are foremost among them.

To conclude this section on the significance and the centrality of love, we look to Augustine's *Enchiridion on Faith, Hope, and Charity*, in which he singles out love (i.e., charity) as the greatest of the theological virtues:

> Now, as for charity, which the apostle [Paul] says is greater than the other two, that is faith and hope [cf. 1 Corinthians 13:13], the greater it is in a person, the better that person in whom it is. For

12. Augustine, *Homilies on the First Epistle of John*, 10.3.

13. See Augustine, 10.3: "When you love Christ's members . . . you love Christ; when you love Christ, you love the Son of God; when you love the Son of God, you also love his Father. Love, then, cannot be separated."

> when we ask whether somebody is a good person, we are not asking what he believes or what he hopes for but what he loves. For one who rightly loves without doubt rightly believes and hopes, and one who does not love believes in vain, even if the things he believes are true; he hopes in vain, even if the things for which he hopes are those which . . . belong to true happiness, unless he also believes and hopes that if he asks he may also be given the ability to love.[14]

All the theological virtues are gifts of God, infused virtues resulting from God's bestowal of grace upon us. Love alone, though, endures forever. By clinging to God as our eternal, everlasting good, we have an object of love that cannot be taken away from us, either now or when this mortal life is over. For Augustine, love of God is the happiness he has been seeking from the earliest of his extant writings onward. Thus, since happiness is the final end of all things, all things must in turn be ordered to love of God as their final end. With this general account of love in mind, let us turn now to Augustine's *Confessions.*

CONFESSIONS

In the opening lines of *Confessions*, Augustine presents in microcosm the journey narrated and performed in the work as a whole:

> Great are you, O Lord, and exceedingly worthy of praise [cf. Psalm 47:2(48:1); 95(96):4; 144(145):3]; your power is immense, and your wisdom beyond reckoning. And so we humans, who are a due part of your creation, long to praise you—we who carry

14. Augustine, *Enchiridion*, 31.117, in *The Augustine Catechism: The Enchiridion on Faith, Hope, and Charity*, trans. Bruce Harbert, ed. Boniface Ramsey, vol. 1 of *The Works of St. Augustine* (Hyde Park, NY: New City Press, 1999). Unless otherwise indicated, all quotations of the *Enchiridion* are from this edition.

our mortality about with us, carry the evidence of our sin and with it the proof that you thwart the proud. Yet these humans, due part of your creation as they are, still do long to praise you. You stir us so that praising you may bring us joy, because you have made us and drawn us to yourself, and our heart is unquiet until it rests in you.[15]

A great deal could be said about these opening lines, but for our purposes we will focus on those elements that most pertain to our study of Augustine's philosophy and theology of education.[16]

All the theological virtues are gifts of God, infused virtues resulting from God's bestowal of grace upon us. Love alone, though, endures forever. By clinging to God as our eternal, everlasting good, we have an object of love that cannot be taken away from us, either now or when this mortal life is over. For Augustine, love of God is the happiness he has been seeking from the earliest of his extant writings onward. Thus since happiness is the final end of all things, all things must in turn be ordered to love of God as their final end.

First, note how Augustine begins the work not with his own words, but with a citation from the Bible, the written Word of God. From the beginning, Augustine sees himself and his journey as in essence "authored" by God, man's source and origin as well as his final

15. Augustine, *Confessions*, 1.1.1.

16. For a more detailed account of the opening lines, see my article: " 'As I read, I was set on fire': On the Psalms in Augustine's *Confessions*," *LOGOS: A Journal of Catholic Thought and Culture* 16, no. 2 (Spring 2013), 160–184 (esp. 165–168).

end. Direct quotations from Sacred Scripture abound in *Confessions*. Significantly, Augustine considers his life as ultimately intelligible only in light of God and his providential purposes for the entire created order; since the principal source of Augustine's knowledge of God and his ways is the Bible, he takes his bearings throughout *Confessions* from the written Word of God. Furthermore, since Augustine's own personal journey is presented as a paradigm for every man's journey, he invites his readers to render their own lives intelligible by considering them in light of what the Bible has to say about God's existence and his plans for them. God is man's Author and Teacher, the One who brings man into existence, continually sustains him, directs him throughout life, and offers to receive him back into eternal fellowship even after man has fallen headlong into sin.

This manner of beginning also sheds light on the work's title. Not only is the opening line a quotation from the Bible; these words are also from the Psalter, the "prayer book of the Church" through which man learns how to praise God. In Augustine's writings, the term *confession* is typically used in one of two senses: either as a confession of sin or as a confession of praise. As *Confessions* unfolds, we come to see that for Augustine an essential part of man's vocation in this life and the next is confessing the praises of God.[17] Praising God is a manifestation of man's love for his Creator and Redeemer.

---

17. In his *Exposition of the Psalms*, a series of individual reflections on all 150 psalms, Augustine meditates extensively on the nature and purpose of confession. In his exposition on Psalm 99 (100), while commenting on the verse, "Enter his gates with thanksgiving" (v. 4), he says the following:

> Let the flock come in through the gates. . . . And how is it to get in? By confession. Confession must be your gateway, your beginning. . . . And once we are inside, shall we not continue to confess? Yes, indeed; confess always, for you always have reason to confess. It can hardly happen that any one of us is in this life so changed that nothing blameworthy remains; you need to rebuke yourself, lest he rebuke you, he who must condemn you. Once you have entered his courts, then, confess to him. When will there be no place for the confession of sins? Only in that rest which awaits us, where we shall be [like] the angels. But notice that I said, "There will be no place then for the confession of sins." I did not say, "There will be no place for confession"; for confession there will be, the confession of praise. You will confess forever that he is God, and you his creature. (Augustine, *Expositions of the Psalms [99–120]*, trans. Maria Boulding, OSB, vol. 19 of *The Works of St. Augustine* [Hyde Park, NY: New City Press, 2003], 99.16)

Indeed, Augustine conceives of the writing of *Confessions* itself as a "sacrifice of praise" offered to God before Augustine's readers.[18] And as Augustine has been taught how to praise God through a meditative reading of the psalms, he in turn seeks to teach his readers to do the same: to confess their sins and to confess praise to God for his goodness toward and providential care for them. In describing his retreat at Cassiciacum, Augustine gives us a glimpse of such meditative reading and its effect on him:

> How loudly I cried out to you, my God, as I read the psalms of David, songs full of faith, outbursts of devotion with no room in them for the breath of pride! Uncouth I was in real love for you. . . . How loudly I began to cry out to you in those psalms, how I was inflamed by them with love for you and fired to recite them to the whole world, were I able, as a remedy against human pride![19]

As Augustine has been taught how to praise God through a meditative reading of the psalms, he in turn seeks to teach his readers to do the same: to confess their sins and to confess praise to God for his goodness toward and providential care for them.

As yet "uncouth in real love" for God, Augustine looks to the psalms for inspiration. As he meditatively reads them (in the context immediately following, he meditates on Psalm 4), he is "inflamed . . . with love for [God] and fired to recite them to the whole world." As several readers have pointed out, this "recitation" is exactly what he does—*figuratively* speaking—in writing

18. See, for example, Augustine, *Confessions*, 8.1.1., cf. Psalm 115 (116): 16-17.
19. Augustine, 9.4.8.

Confessions. Given the preponderance of biblical quotations contained therein, it is clear that reading through Augustine's *Confessions* is meant to provide an occasion for his readers to follow him on this meditative journey. As a master teacher, Augustine does not simply point the way; he walks with us, sharing the journey with us as we proceed together toward happiness in God. In addition to engendering love, such reading also serves as a remedy against human pride—the very fault presented in the opening lines as the besetting sin of mankind.

As a master teacher, Augustine does not simply point the way; he walks with us, sharing the journey with us as we proceed together toward happiness in God.

Considering *Confessions* as a whole, there are three related themes to which we should attend before moving on. First, as one might guess from what has been said thus far, teaching and learning are central themes throughout the work. Augustine speaks of the joys and sufferings of learning at the hands of good and bad teachers. His early teachers of grammar and rhetoric lead him away from God, immersing him instead in a pursuit of the things and ways of this world: power, prestige, wealth, etc. Nevertheless, God uses even the worst of Augustine's experiences and the most dubious intentions of his teachers (and of Augustine himself) to lead Augustine back to him. Furthermore, Augustine learns under the fatherly care of Bishop Ambrose, even though Ambrose never serves as a formal teacher to Augustine. Eventually, these good and bad teachers, as well as good and bad teachings, lead Augustine to acknowledge Christ as his true and "Inner Teacher."[20] Among many other things, Augustine singles out learning humility and charity (love) from Christ's Incarnation.[21]

Instead of passions being inherently opposed to reason, Augustine sees rightly ordered passions as wholly natural and indeed allied to reason in the ascent of the mind and heart to God.

Second, Augustine presents the story of his journey as an ordering of his desires and a purification and perfection of his loves. Rather than seeing desires as subhuman, deriving from man's "animal" nature, Augustine narrates his maturation at least in part as a learning of how to prudently judge his desires—uprooting some, purifying others, and even feeding those that are rightly ordered. As in the passage above on reading the psalms, Augustine frequently speaks of being "inflamed" by what he reads or hears. Instead of passions being inherently opposed to reason, Augustine sees rightly ordered passions as wholly natural and indeed allied to reason in the ascent of the mind and heart to God. When Augustine reflects upon his reasons for writing *Confessions*, he says that his principal intention was to "draw a person's mind and

---

20. See Augustine, 5.6.10:

> For some time, though, you had been teaching me in wondrous, hidden ways, my God (and I believe that you taught me because it is true; there is no other teacher of truth except you, though teachers aplenty have made a name for themselves in many a place); so I had already learned under your tuition that nothing should be regarded as true because it is eloquently stated, nor false because the words sound clumsy.

For the definitive statement of Augustine's doctrine of Christ as the "Inner Teacher," see *De magistro* (*The Teacher*), 11.38 ff.

21. Augustine presents humility and charity as the beginning and end, respectively, of his journey toward happiness in God. In describing the effect of reading the books of the Platonists, Augustine says to God, "You wanted to show me first and foremost how you thwart the proud but give grace to the humble, and with what immense mercy on your part the way of humility was demonstrated to us when your Word was made flesh and dwelt among men and women" (*Confessions*, 7.9.13). For all the good that reading the books of the Platonists does Augustine by leading him to knowledge of immaterial being, they nevertheless lack charity (*Confessions*, 7.20.26), without which, as we have seen, Augustine thinks the happy life cannot be possessed.

emotions towards [God]."[22] We will have more to say about the ordering of loves when discussing *City of God* below.

By teaching the people of God about the divine plan for the created order and man's privileged place within it, Augustine is helping to bring himself and his readers toward the hoped-for eternal rest in God.

Third and finally, the entire structure of *Confessions* can profitably be viewed in terms of Augustine's growth to the full stature of a teacher who rightly speaks with truth *and* eloquence. In his early years of education, Augustine is surrounded by teachers who care deeply about eloquence but little (if at all) about truth. In terms of teaching, Augustine's encounter with Ambrose is a turning point. Augustine presents the teachings of Ambrose as a synthesis of truth and eloquence, a synthesis that Augustine makes his aspiration for the remainder of his life. In the final three books of *Confessions*, Augustine enters into an extended commentary on the opening chapters of Genesis. Inspired by what Ambrose had taught him about biblical interpretation, Augustine, as a Catholic bishop, teaches his readers the entire course of salvation history from these opening chapters. Contrary to what some scholars have thought, then, the last three books are a fitting conclusion to *Confessions* as a whole when considered from a pedagogical point of view. They situate the narrative of Augustine's own life within the whole of salvation history, and they afford Augustine the opportunity to exercise his gifts as an expositor and teacher of God's Word for the good of the Body of Christ.[23] By teaching the people of God about the divine plan for the created order

22. Augustine, *Revisions*, 2.6.

23. Incidentally, the final three books shed significant light upon why Augustine refers to "our heart" in the opening lines of *Confessions*. The "heart" he has in mind is not his own (or any other individual man's), but that of the Body of Christ, his Church, which is presented in the final book of *Confessions* as that for the sake of which God created all things.

and man's privileged place within it, Augustine is helping to bring himself and his readers toward the hoped-for eternal rest in God.

City of God

Excluding his *Expositions of the Psalms* (which Augustine never intended to be a unified treatise with a central argument), *City of God* is his longest, most comprehensive work. For centuries it was considered "the classical expression of Christian political thought and of the Christian attitude to history."[24] The title was inspired by Psalm 87(86):3—"Glorious things are spoken of you, O city of God" (RSV)—perhaps an ironic reply to the slanderous accusations that pagans were making against Christianity at the time. Begun soon after the sack of Rome by Alaric and the Visigoths in 410, *City of God* was written in part as a response to pagan detractors who faulted Christianity for the disaster.[25] Augustine divided the work broadly into two parts. Books I–X are a response to the charges of pagan detractors, and books XI–XXII offer a positive account of the Christian faith and its proper relation to things of this world. The latter part is subdivided into three sections, dedicated respectively to the origin (XI–XIV), development (XV–XVIII), and end (XIX–XXII) of two "cities": the City of God, symbolized by Jerusalem, and the Earthly City, symbolized by Babylon. As mentioned in

24. Ernest L. Fortin, s.v. "*Civitate Dei, De*," in *Augustine through the Ages*, 196–202.

25. See Fortin, 197. Fortin argues that there were really two different arguments made by pagans against the Christians. According to the first, a popular argument "on the street," Rome's greatness was due to the favor of the pagan gods. By accepting Christianity and rejecting paganism, Rome had incurred the wrath of these gods and lost their protection. The present calamity was a judgment of Jove, an act of revenge. The pagan elite, however, had long since abandoned any serious belief in Roman mythology. The likes of Varro, Seneca, and Cicero all dissembled, publicly engaging in religious rituals while privately disbelieving (and for some, even detesting) pagan religion. The second, more serious argument was that the rise of Christianity brought about a decline in public spiritedness and thus was indirectly responsible for the deterioration of the Roman Empire. In any event, our principal concern here is with the latter portion of the work, which outlines the origin, development, and end of the two cities.

chapter 3, these two cities are characterized by their loves: the City of God by the love of God to the contempt of oneself, and the Earthly City by the love of oneself to the contempt of God.[26]

Before we proceed, a few words of clarification need to be said about Augustine's division of men and angels into two cities. First, these cities are *not* "empirical entities."[27] That is to say, they are not cities in the ordinary, physical sense, but in a mystical sense.[28] Citizenship in one of these cities is based upon the object of one's love, the ultimate end toward which one's actions are directed.[29] Thus membership in one city or the other is not unalterably determined until death. Furthermore, the City of God and the Earthly City are inextricably mixed in this life and will remain so until Judgment Day.[30] Before that time, those who are part of the City of God are unknown to us. Not everyone who is a member of the Catholic Church and outwardly adheres to her teachings belongs to the City of God; and many who are not formally affiliated with the Church may nonetheless be part of the City of God. The same ignorance of "who's in and who's out" holds, of course, for the Earthly City, since we have no external way of knowing whether any particular individual is truly virtuous or not. Regarding the City of God, it is established in heaven,[31] and its perfect realization will come only at the end of time after the Final Judgment. Nonetheless, the City

26. The Earthly City lives according to the "flesh" (see Galatians 5) and is guided by self-love. The principal delusion of the earthly citizen is a proud presumption of total independence and self-sufficiency. This delusion gives rise to the basic characteristic of the Earthly City: "to worship a god or gods so that with their assistance it may reign in the enjoyment of victories and an earthly peace, not with a loving concern for others, but with lust for domination over them" (Augustine, *City of God*, 15.7). In the City of God, on the other hand, "humility is highly prized . . . and especially enjoined [upon its citizens] during the time of its pilgrimage in this world; and it [i.e., humility] receives particular emphasis in the character of Christ, the king of that City" (Augustine, 14.13).

27. Fortin, "*Civitate Dei, De*," 196.

28. Augustine, *City of God*, 15.1.

29. Augustine, 14.28. For another notable summary of the two cities and their respective loves, see also Augustine's *On the Literal Meaning of Genesis*, 11.15.

30. Augustine explains this reality in terms of the parable of the weeds among the wheat (Matthew 13:24-30).

31. Due to this, Augustine often calls the City of God the "Heavenly City."

of God begins here and now insofar as human beings assent to the teaching of Christ and by God's grace lead virtuous lives.

With these introductory comments behind us, let us turn to a few central themes of *City of God* that will help to develop our understanding of key elements of Augustine's account of education.

First, in *City of God* Augustine speaks once again of God as teacher: "Our nature has God as its author; and so without doubt we must have him as our teacher, if we are to attain true wisdom; and for our happiness we require him as the bestower of the delight in our hearts which only he can give."[32] Given that God is our creator, says Augustine, we must look to him to know the path to true wisdom since he made us and thus established the end (or purpose) for our nature; only through his gifts may our hearts receive their deepest desire. In another passage, Augustine identifies the Teacher's central precepts: "Now God, our master, teaches two chief precepts, love of God and love of neighbour; and in them man finds three objects for his love: God, himself, and his neighbour; and a man who loves God is not wrong in loving himself."[33] We will return to these central teachings when discussing *On Christian Teaching* below.

Second, *City of God* sheds additional light on the importance of ordering our loves. As Augustine explains,

> If the Creator is truly loved, that is, if he himself is loved, and not something else in his stead, then he cannot be wrongly loved. We must, in fact, observe the right order even in our love for the very love with which we love what is deserving of love, so that there may be in us the virtue which is the condition of the good life. Hence, as it seems to me, a brief and true definition of virtue is "rightly ordered love."[34]

32. Augustine, *City of God*, 11.25.

33. Augustine, 19.14.

34. Augustine, 15.22.

We saw earlier that for Augustine, all virtues are forms of love. Here he defines virtue as rightly ordered love. In *Confessions* as well as in *City of God*, setting one's loves in order is the central condition for progress in the happy life. Moreover, this ordering of loves prepares one for incorporation into the Body of Christ. Augustine defines a "people" as "the association of a multitude of rational beings united by a common agreement on the objects of their love."[35] The people of the City of God are a community of ordered loves, a community that has God as the ultimate object of its love and that orders all other loves with respect to this first love. In the final book of *City of God*, Augustine identifies the goal of the Heavenly City. Drawing upon St. Paul's account of Christ and his Body as the "perfection of manhood" or "mature manhood" in Ephesians 4, Augustine says that the mature Christ—i.e., Christ the Head united eternally with his Body, the Church—is the final and perfect state of the City of God. This perfected state is attained through the building up of the Body of Christ in rightly ordered love.[36]

Finally, whereas in *Confessions* Augustine speaks of the perfected state of the Body of Christ principally in terms of *rest*, here in *City of God* he casts it in terms of the more corporate, political notion of *peace*, but with occasional reference to rest (or "repose") to describe the nature of that peace. Construing peace generally as a "harmony of congruous elements,"[37] Augustine offers a comprehensive picture of peace in terms of the establishment of God's order throughout Creation:

> The peace of the body . . . is a tempering of the component parts in duly ordered proportion; the peace of the irrational soul is a duly ordered repose of the appetites; the peace of the rational soul is the duly ordered agreement of cognition and action.

35. Augustine, 19.24.
36. Augustine, 22.18.
37. Augustine, 19.12.

> The peace of body and soul is the duly ordered life and health of a living creature; peace between mortal man and God is an ordered obedience, in faith, in subjection to an [eternal] law; peace between men is the ordered agreement among those who live together about giving and obeying orders; the peace of the Heavenly City is a perfectly ordered and perfectly harmonious fellowship in the enjoyment of God, and a mutual fellowship in God; the peace of the whole universe is the tranquility of order—and order is the arrangement of things equal and unequal in a pattern which assigns to each its proper position.[38]

Note well that in this all-embracing vision of peace, the "harmony of congruous parts" on one level, while good in itself, is also ordered and conducive to peace on the next level. Thus, for example, worldly political peace among men is ordered and conducive to the peace of the City of God.[39] In light of this grand vision, it should not be surprising that Augustine says our ultimate desire is for peace:

> As it is . . . human nature has refused to keep that peace with God in happiness; and so in its unhappiness it is at war with itself. . . . Our desire is, indeed, to be free even of this war; and by the fire of divine love we are set on fire with longing to attain that orderly peace where the lower elements may be subdued to the higher in a stability that can never be shaken.[40]

This "fire of divine love" is kindled in our hearts by the Holy Spirit, the third Person of the Holy Trinity. To attain peace—that "stability that can never be shaken"—we must be reconciled to

---

38. Augustine, 19.13.

39. Contrary to a common caricature of Augustine's political thought, he is neither uninterested nor disdainful of secular political order. In fact, for Augustine such order is certainly beneficial to the establishment of higher levels of peace and order. While peace among and within nations is not required for the peace of the City of God, it is nevertheless something to be prayed for and sought, regardless of how successful we may be in attaining it.

40. Augustine, *City of God*, 21.15.

the God in whose image we have been created. In order to further explore this theme, we turn now to Augustine's work *On the Trinity*.

On the Trinity

Augustine composed *On the Trinity* gradually over a period of more than twenty years (399–419). Much to his annoyance, some of the "books" of the work were published separately without his consent before he had completed the whole work. In a letter to Aurelius, then bishop of Carthage, Augustine insists upon the unity of the work: "It had been my intention to publish them [i.e., the books of *On the Trinity*] all together and not one by one, because the inquiry proceeds in a closely-knit development from the first of them to the last."[41]

Although this "closely-knit development" may not be readily apparent to a first-time reader, *On the Trinity* is nevertheless indeed carefully wrought. The work as a whole gives an account of man's ascent to participation in the divine life of the Holy Trinity, an ascent that may begin in this life but which finds its consummation in the eternal blessed state. This account has four basic parts.[42] In the first part (books I–IV), Augustine considers the foundation for man's participatory ascent, namely that Jesus Christ and the Holy Spirit—as they are manifested in the Old and New Testaments—are coequal with God the Father. In the second part (books V–VII), he examines the ways in which the New Testament authors employ names to signify the divine unity as well as the distinction among the "persons" of the Trinity.[43] Then, beginning with justice and truth as indicators of our participation in the divine light of God,

41. Augustine, *On the Trinity* (*The Trinity* trans.), Prefatory Letter.

42. Throughout this section, I am indebted to the clear and concise treatment of *On the Trinity* found in Matthew Levering's *The Theology of Augustine: An Introductory Guide to His Most Important Works* (Grand Rapids, MI: Baker Academic, 2013), 151–186.

43. See Levering, 152: "If we do not understand this naming, we will not be able to gain insight into the God who is named or participate in him through Christ and the Spirit."

Augustine proceeds in the third part (books VIII–XV) to identify created images through which we may ascend to contemplate the unity of God as well as the aforementioned distinction among the persons of the Trinity. In the final books (XII–XV), Augustine draws together the image of God in man (from the third part) with the account of the missions of God the Son and God the Spirit (from the first part) in order to reveal the highest possible way of participating in the Trinity during this life, namely "contemplation of the Triune God in and through the created image purified by the missions [of the Son and Spirit]."[44] Matthew Levering summarizes the purpose of the work as follows: "*On the Trinity* seeks to understand and to model what Christian life is all about. For Christians, the ascent to participation in God begins now: through the grace of the Holy Spirit, in faith and love, we are being conformed to the image of Jesus Christ, perfect wisdom and perfect love."[45]

Regarding Augustine as master teacher, we can learn several things from *On the Trinity*. First, as was the case in *Confessions* and *City of God*, Augustine's teaching is grounded in the Bible: "The purpose of all the Catholic commentators I have been able to read on the divine books of both testaments, who have written before me on the [T]rinity which God is, has been to teach that according to the [S]criptures Father and Son and Holy Spirit in the inseparable equality of one substance present a divine unity."[46] Relying upon the tradition of Catholic commentary on Scripture, Augustine bases his account of the Trinity on key passages from the Old and New Testaments. At the same time, Augustine also draws heavily upon his training in and study of the best of Greco-Roman thought. One conspicuous example of this is his discussion in the second part of

44. Note well that "Book 15 includes reflection on the weakness of the image, not to show that we do not participate in the Trinity through the created image purified by the missions, but to show that our participation in this life should be ever-increasing but cannot attain anything near the vision that will be given to us in eternal life" (Levering, 152).

45. Levering, 152.

46. Augustine, *On the Trinity* (*The Trinity* trans.), 1.2.7.

how to distinguish the names of God that refer to his "one-ness" from those that signify his "three-ness." Augustine focuses on Exodus 3:14, where in response to Moses's question God names himself as "I am who I am" (RSV). Based on this text, Augustine argues that God's being is infinite and thus immutable. While God's *substance* may never change, Augustine contends that there can be—indeed, there are—*relations* in God; nonetheless, these relations do not change his substance in any way. In making his case, Augustine relies upon the distinctions Aristotle makes in his *Categories* between substance and the nine "accidents" (or attributes). Whatever is said of God's substance remains always the same and pertains to all three persons of the Trinity; God the Father, God the Son, and God the Holy Spirit are distinct only in relation to one another and not in their substance.

Augustine also uses the notion of "turning around"—a concept present in the Judeo-Christian tradition (as religious "conversion") as well as the Greco-Roman tradition (as a philosophical "turning" away from lower things toward higher)—in order to articulate the need for a new perspective: "God sent us sights suited to our wandering state, to admonish us that what we seek is not here, and that we must turn back from the things around us to where our whole being springs from."[47] This turning inward, away from the things of this world and toward a contemplation of man's own nature, is crucial to the contemplative ascent that Augustine teaches in this work. In the third part of *On the Trinity*, he considers various "triads" that arise from a contemplation of human nature in light of the Trinity. Among these, the act of love exhibits the triad of lover, beloved, and love. In analyzing this triad, Augustine comes upon another: the mind, the mind's knowledge of itself, and the mind's love of itself. Augustine also explores memory, understanding, and will as well as various bodily triads:[48] "As presented by Augustine,

47. Augustine, 3.26.2.

48. For example, in the act of seeing there is a visible object, our vision of the object, and our intention to see the object.

these triads constitute a movement inward, an ascent from the material world toward the spiritual, that leads toward the full participatory image of the Trinity: mind, knowledge, and love."[49] Significantly, Augustine describes our contemplation of these triads as "a ladder for those who would climb to happiness."[50] The turn inward gives rise to a turn upward, enabling Augustine to ascend toward his Creator, in whose image man is made. Thus the God who is Love inspires Augustine to contemplate love in order to know God and to know himself. As Augustine proceeds in the third part of *On the Trinity* to investigate what it means to say that man is made in the image of God, his meditations on divine and human love lead him to greater insight regarding human nature.

The turn inward gives rise to a turn upward, enabling Augustine to ascend toward his Creator, in whose image man is made. Thus the God who is Love inspires Augustine to contemplate love in order to know God and to know himself.

A final point, closely related to the last, is the importance of Christ and the Incarnation in Augustine's intellectual ascent. In the fourth part of the work, Augustine engages in an inquiry about whether—and if so, how—we may participate intellectually in the Trinity, both in this life as well as in the next. Central to his account is the distinction between *scientia* and *sapientia*. When the mind knows itself, it achieves *scientia*, or the knowledge of created things; when contemplating the triune nature of God, the mind rises to *sapientia*, or true wisdom. Since Christ is fully God and fully man, he bridges for us the gap between *scientia* and *sapientia*:

49. Levering, *The Theology of Augustine*, 171. Clearly, the inward turn here is likely the same sort of inward turn Augustine makes in *Confessions*.

50. Augustine, *On the Trinity* (*The Trinity* trans.), 11.3.10.

> Our knowledge therefore is Christ, and our wisdom is the same Christ. It is he who plants faith in us about temporal things, he who presents us with the truth about eternal things. Through him we go straight toward him, through knowledge [*scientia*] toward wisdom [*sapientia*], without ever turning aside from one and the same Christ, *in whom are hidden all the treasures of wisdom and knowledge* [Colossians 2:3].[51]

On Christian Teaching

Augustine composed most of *On Christian Teaching*, which consists of a preface and four books, in 396 and 397; later, in 426, he extended the third book and added the fourth. Although Augustine had long since abandoned his earlier career as an orator and professor of rhetoric, as a Catholic priest and later as a bishop he continued to have a need to practice the rhetorical art—especially as an interpreter and preacher of Sacred Scripture. The influence of *On Christian Teaching* on the Western tradition of both preaching and rhetoric has been remarkable.[52] In this work, "Augustine begins rhetoric anew within the tradition of Christian thought, but he simultaneously draws on the classical thought of

51. Augustine, 13.6.24. Noting the centrality of Christ in Augustine's meditative ascent is not meant to downplay the role of the Holy Spirit in any way. As Levering rightly points out, "The missions of the Son *and the Holy Spirit* restore the mind's ability to remember, know, and love itself as a participation in the eternal divine mind" (Levering, *The Theology of Augustine*, 180 [emphasis added]). My purpose in the current context is simply to point out another way in which Augustine's philosophy and theology of education are fundamentally informed by his understanding of the Incarnation and its influence on man's knowledge of himself and of God.

52. As James J. Murphy puts it, "It is interesting to note that the first rhetorical work to be printed in the fifteenth century was not one of Aristotle or of Cicero, but rather book 4 of Saint Augustine's [*On Christian Teaching*]. . . . Also, it is worth noting that hardly any of the three hundred preaching manuals composed during the Middle Ages have ever reached print at all; most remain in manuscript to this day" (Murphy, "Foreword," *The Rhetoric of St. Augustine of Hippo:* De Doctrina Christiana *and the Search for a Distinctly Christian Rhetoric*, ed. Richard Leo Enos, et al. [Waco, TX: Baylor University Press, 2008], xi). *On Christian Teaching* enjoyed continuous popularity throughout the Middle Ages and during the Renaissance.

Isocrates and Cicero in seeking to unite wisdom and eloquence."[53] Augustine's central themes are biblical interpretation and preaching.[54] The organizing principle of the work is the love of God and the love of neighbor for God's sake. In interpreting Scripture, Augustine identifies two essential tasks: discovering the truth to be learned and teaching the truth discovered to others.

Augustine begins his account by distinguishing between things and signs. *Things* are the individual instances of various natures that we encounter: sheep, trees, stones, etc. *Signs* (verbal and written) are those words by means of which we learn about things. In addition, God and human beings use some things themselves as signs for other things. Augustine spends the remainder of the first book discussing things. Within this context, he makes a distinction between using and enjoying things:

> So then, there are some things which are meant to be enjoyed, others which are meant to be used, yet others which do both the enjoying and the using. Things that are to be enjoyed make us happy; things which are to be used help us on our way to happiness. . . . We ourselves, however, both enjoy and use things, and find ourselves in the middle, in a position to choose which to do.[55]

Augustine's distinction between "to use" (*uti*) and "to enjoy" (*frui*), a distinction that is also present in all the major works we have considered, has been much maligned and misunderstood.[56]

---

53. Amy K. Hermanson, et al., "Saint Augustine and the Creation of a Distinctly Christian Rhetoric," in *The Rhetoric of St. Augustine of Hippo*, xi.

54. Speaking of *On Christian Teaching*, Augustine summarizes the four books as follows: "The first three are useful for understanding the [S]criptures, while the fourth is about how things that we understand should be set forth" (*Revisions*, 2.4).

55. Augustine, *Teaching Christianity (De Doctrina Christiana)*, trans. Edmund Hill, OP, vol. 11 of *The Works of St. Augustine* (Hyde Park, NY: New City Press, 2010), 1.3.3. Unless otherwise indicated, all quotations of *Teaching Christianity* (more commonly known as *On Christian Teaching*) are from this edition.

56. For example, some fault Augustine with "instrumentalizing" everything but God, since all else is to be "used" and not "enjoyed." This objection, however, fundamentally misunderstands how Augustine is employing the terms *uti* and *frui*.

As Levering rightly argues, for Augustine, "To enjoy a thing is to cleave to it with all our heart. When we seek a thing in order to enjoy it, we make it our ultimate happiness and we consider it the resting point of our desire."[57] To use a thing, on the other hand, is to treat it not as the ultimate object of our happiness, but as something that can help us to attain that happiness. Augustine introduces the distinction between *use* and *enjoyment* to underscore the fundamental importance of rightly ordered love:

> Living a just and holy life requires one to be capable of an objective and impartial evaluation of things; to love things, that is to say, in the right order, so that you do not love what is not to be loved, or fail to love what is to be loved, or have a greater love for what should be loved less, or an equal love for things that should be loved less or more, or a lesser or greater love for things that should be loved equally.[58]

For Augustine, the entire purpose of Scripture is to teach us rightly ordered love so that we can dwell for all eternity with the Trinity together with the saints. The central biblical text for Augustine on this topic is Matthew 22:37-40: "You shall love the Lord your God with all your heart, and with all your soul, and with all your mind. This is the great and first commandment. And a second is like it, You shall love your neighbor as yourself. On these two commandments depend all the law and the prophets" (RSV). As Augustine interprets this passage, we should love God for his own sake and our neighbor for God's sake. As in *City of God*, Augustine here likens man to a pilgrim—an alien and a stranger—who is seeking to return to his homeland. To become attached through enjoyment to anything but God is to forsake the

57. Levering, *The Theology of Augustine*, 3–4. In his *The Christian Philosophy of Saint Augustine*, Etienne Gilson offers a clear, detailed account of Augustine's argument (165–167). See also Edmund Hill's helpful comments in the aforementioned edition of *The Trinity* (280 n. 24).

58. Augustine, *Teaching Christianity*, 1.28.

journey home. That "home" is the Trinity, and our progress toward this home occurs not through physical movement from place to place, but through the spiritual "movement" of ardent, holy love.[59]

Significantly, Augustine also speaks of Christ as both our physician and the medicine to cure the wound that is sin. Our most basic disease is pride, and the Great Physician applies the cure of humility to heal us. The beginning of our journey back to God is humility. By receiving the cure, renouncing our pride, and regaining the ability to judge things for what they are—either as things to be enjoyed or things to be used—we are enabled to rightly order our loves and return to happiness in God.

To become attached through enjoyment to anything but God is to forsake the journey home. That "home" is the Trinity, and our progress toward this home occurs not through physical movement from place to place, but through the spiritual "movement" of ardent, holy love.

Beyond these general comments on the work, there are three specific elements for us to note. First, Augustine offers helpful advice to preachers on how to read and teach both biblical and pagan texts. Regarding the interpretation of the Bible, Augustine counsels prudence and humility. We should begin with clear passages, and then proceed to more obscure ones. Augustine also distinguishes between literal and figurative words or signs. When unclear, figurative words should be approached through knowledge

---

59. Compare Augustine's description of the nature of his journey back to God in *Confessions*, 8.8.19: "It was a journey not to be undertaken by ship or carriage or on foot, nor need it take me even that short distance I had walked from the house to the place where we were sitting [in the garden]; for to travel—and more, to reach journey's end—was nothing else but to want to go there, but to want it valiantly and with all my heart."

of biblical languages and through knowledge of things. He also advocates "plundering the Egyptians"; that is to say, by appropriating the best aspects of pagan learning, Christian preachers should use these treasures for the love of God and neighbor.[60]

Second, the goal of preaching is for the people of God to hear and understand the truth from Sacred Scripture.[61] Recall that for Augustine, the twin tasks of the preacher are discovering the truth and teaching it to others. Augustine offers biblical examples of eloquence, most notably the prophet Amos and the apostle Paul. For Augustine, rhetorical eloquence always should be at the service of wisdom. Furthermore, while a preacher may not be eloquent, he should be wise. Be that as it may, eloquence can greatly enhance the preacher's ability to teach wisdom effectively; the best preaching unites wisdom and eloquence.

Finally, Augustine places special emphasis on the character of the preacher. While observing the rules of rhetoric is to be expected, Augustine insists on the necessity of prayer before Christian preaching. Only by praying can the preacher be the willing and conscious instrument of God in proclaiming the good news of salvation and sanctification. Augustine concludes

---

60. See Augustine, *Teaching Christianity*, 2.60:

> If those . . . who are called philosophers happen to have said anything that is true, and agreeable to our faith, the Platonists above all, not only should we not be afraid of them, but we should even claim back for our own use what they have said, as from its unjust possessors. It is like the Egyptians, who not only had idols and heavy burdens, which the people of Israel abominated and fled from, but also vessels and ornaments of gold and silver, and fine raiment, which the people secretly appropriated for their own, and indeed better, use as they went forth from Egypt; and this not on their own initiative, but on God's instructions, with the Egyptians unwittingly lending them things they were not themselves making good use of.

In this passage, Augustine is referring to the events of Exodus 11:1-3 and 12:33-36. The concept of "plundering the Egyptians" was used by Christian theologians prior to Augustine, including by St. Irenaeus (130–202), Origen (ca. 184–253), and St. Gregory of Nazianzus (329–390). Even so, Augustine's formulation and defense of the concept arguably has had the greatest impact on later Christian thought and culture.

61. See Levering, *The Theology of Augustine*, 15–16. As Levering explains, for Augustine, "Until the audience has understood, the preacher has not really 'spoken.' The best preaching will be not only direct but also eloquent, because a preacher should teach, delight, and move the audience."

On Christian Teaching by emphasizing the importance of the preacher's living a holy life. Broadening the classical concept of the ethical appeal,[62] Augustine contends that a life well lived is more important than eloquence for persuading an audience. Things (the preacher's life as manifest in his actions and character) are more important than signs (the words of the preacher). Augustine further exhorts the preacher to pray to God for wisdom, in a spirit of gratitude and humility.

62. According to Aristotle in his *Rhetoric*, "Persuasion is achieved by the speaker's personal character [*ethos*] when the speech is so spoken as to make us think him credible" (Aristotle, *The Basic Works of Aristotle*, ed. Richard McKeon [New York: Random House, 1941], 1.2 [1356a4–5]). The emphasis for Aristotle (and the classical tradition of rhetoric up to Augustine's time) is on the character of the speaker insofar as it is manifest during the speech itself, not on the character of the speaker *in general*, as it is for Augustine.

CHAPTER SIX

Augustine's Legacy and Its Relevance Today

In this final chapter, we will explore the legacy of Augustine's philosophy and theology of education, as well as its relevance today. Before we do so, though, we need to put the task before us into perspective. As David Vincent Meconi, SJ, has noted, "After St. Paul, no follower of Jesus Christ has been discussed or written about more than St. Augustine of Hippo."[1] From the time of his conversion to the present day, Augustine's life and writings have been topics of ongoing consideration for philosophers and theologians, historians and poets, clergy and laity. Even in his own lifetime, eminent men recognized how extraordinary Augustine's contributions were. In a letter written to Augustine in 418, his friend St. Jerome, himself a theologian of no mean stature, said, "You are renowned throughout the whole world; Catholics [honor] and look up to you as the restorer of the ancient faith."[2] Along with St. Gregory the Great, St. Jerome, and St. Ambrose, St. Augustine was recognized by Pope Boniface VIII in 1298 as one of the first Doctors (i.e., "Teachers") of the Catholic Church. Furthermore, not only Catholics but also Protestants look to Augustine as a great theologian and teacher. Both Martin Luther—founder of Lutheranism and himself formerly an Augustinian monk—and John Calvin—founder of Calvinism and the most prominent theologian of the Reformed tradition—claim Augustine as an authority on such matters as God's grace,

1. David Vincent Meconi, *Restless Heart: The Confessions of Saint Augustine* (San Francisco: Ignatius Press, 2013), 2. (This is a booklet that accompanies the recent film of the same name.)
2. Jerome, Epistle 195: From Jerome to Augustine (A.D. 418), http://capress.link/aug0601.

original sin, and divine predestination. Even those outside the Christian faith look to Augustine as an original thinker on philosophical themes such as the nature of time, human memory and consciousness, and freedom of will and human agency. Today, by one scholar's estimate, there are over three hundred scholarly books and articles dedicated to Augustine's life and writings published each year.[3] Similar to Alfred North Whitehead's famous claim that the European philosophical tradition consists of a series of footnotes to Plato, according to Jaroslav Pelikan the history of Western thought from late antiquity up to the Middle Ages and beyond is a series of footnotes to Augustine.[4]

From the time of his conversion, Augustine's life and writings have been topics of ongoing consideration for philosophers and theologians, historians and poets, clergy and laity, into the present day.

Given these facts, any attempt here to provide a sufficient, much less an exhaustive, account of Augustine's legacy and relevance would be a fool's errand. What follows is instead a modest sampling of strands of influence, drawing attention to key figures and themes.[5] In the first half of the chapter, to speak to the legacy of Augustine's philosophy and theology of education, we will consider three figures who were formatively influenced by Augustine: Boethius (ca. 480–524), Hugh of St. Victor (ca. 1096–1141), and Thomas Aquinas (1225–1274). Each of these figures is chosen because of the way he

3. Topping, *St. Augustine*, 3.

4. Jaroslav Pelikan, *The Emergence of the Catholic Tradition (100–600)*, vol. 1 of *The Christian Tradition: A History of the Development of Doctrine* (Chicago: University of Chicago Press, 1971), 330.

5. For a highly recommended (though still admittedly cursory) treatment, see Topping, *St. Augustine*, 111–173.

appropriated and passed on key elements of Augustine's educational theory and practice. In the second portion of the chapter, we will focus on what is arguably Augustine's greatest potential contribution to education today: namely, his teachings on the liberal arts and liberal education.

Augustine's Legacy: Boethius, Hugh of St. Victor, and Thomas Aquinas

Boethius

Presented as a dialogue between Lady Philosophy and Boethius himself, *The Consolation of Philosophy* was written in 523 while Boethius was imprisoned and awaiting trial (and eventual execution) for allegedly committing treason against King Theodoric of the Ostrogoths. The popularity of *The Consolation of Philosophy* from the Carolingian Renaissance through the High Middle Ages was enormous. Read by poets, statesmen, historians, philosophers, and theologians, *Consolation* had a profound philosophical influence on Western thought for centuries. It was so formative of the thought of the medieval world that, according to C. S. Lewis, "To acquire a taste for [*The Consolation of Philosophy*] is almost to become naturalised in the Middle Ages."[6]

6. C. S. Lewis, *The Discarded Image: An Introduction to Medieval and Renaissance Literature* (Cambridge: Cambridge University Press, 1964), 75.

In addition to many literary borrowings, there are unmistakable philosophical connections, such as Augustine's account of time and eternity in Confessions *and the treatment given by Boethius of the same in* Consolation.

As any reader of *Consolation* who has also read Augustine's major works can testify, the influence of Augustine's thought on Boethius is manifest throughout the dialogue.[7] One obvious connection is that the inner dialogue between Augustine and Reason in his *Soliloquies* foreshadows and most likely serves as the literary pattern for the dialogue between Boethius and Lady Philosophy. There is also abundant evidence throughout *Consolation* of such literary dependence upon both Augustine's Cassiciacum dialogues and *Confessions*.[8] In addition to many literary borrowings, there are unmistakable philosophical connections, such as Augustine's account of time and eternity in *Confessions* and the treatment given by Boethius of the same in *Consolation*.[9] These reflections on time and eternity became a major contribution to the continuing discussion of these philosophical topics in the later Western tradition, often included alongside the views of Plato, Aristotle, Kant, Husserl, Heidegger, and others in studies on the philosophy of time.[10] What is more, Boethius also follows Augustine in his emphasis on the liberal arts and their foundational role in liberal education. Boethius himself coins the term *quadrivium* in his

7. For an excellent translation with notes that draw attention to the indebtedness of Boethius to various works of Augustine, especially *Confessions* and *On the Trinity*, see Boethius, *The Consolation of Philosophy*, ed. and trans. Scott Goins and Barbara H. Wyman, Ignatius Critical Editions (San Francisco: Ignatius Press, 2012).

8. See Anne-Marie Bowery, s.v. "Boethius," in *Augustine through the Ages*, 108.

9. See Seamus O'Neill, "Augustine and Boethius, Memory and Eternity," *Analecta Hermeneutica* 6 (2014): 1–20.

10. For example, see Eva Brann's *What, Then, Is Time?* (Lanham, MD: Rowman and Littlefield, 1999).

work *De arithmetica*, and he makes ample use of the liberal arts in *The Consolation of Philosophy*, employing them as means to free himself from preoccupation with temporal things and to turn his gaze to eternal things.[11]

Hugh of St. Victor

Often called "*secundus Augustinus*" ("a second Augustine"), Hugh of St. Victor was formatively influenced by Augustine's thought, both in terms of his theology in general, with its emphasis on the primacy of love, and in terms of his views on the liberal arts and their relation to philosophy and theology.[12]

Today, Hugh is probably best known for his *Didascalicon: De studio legendi*. Put simply, his purpose in writing the book was to offer a practical guide to reading, one that considers *how* one should read as well *what* one should read and *why* one should

11. For an account of his use of dialectic in particular, see my "Lady Philosophy as Physician" in Boethius, *The Consolation of Philosophy*, 187–211. The extent of Boethius's indebtedness to Augustine regarding the liberal arts in particular is difficult to assess given Boethius's extensive exposure to other works and authors, such as Aristotle's treatises on logic, Porphyry's *Isagoge*, Nicomachus's work on arithmetic, etc. Boethius translated many of these works, so his reliance upon these authors is obvious. Nevertheless, we know that Boethius was deeply indebted to Augustine in *Consolation*, and Boethius explicitly acknowledges his debt to Augustine in his work on the Trinity (pref., 30). It is very likely, then, that Boethius learned from his teacher about the liberal arts as well. In his magisterial book on Boethius, Henry Chadwick, a scholar of both figures, says, "I have . . . found more affinity with Augustine than has been generally recognized, and therefore conclude with a portrait of Boethius simultaneously more deeply Neoplatonic and more deeply Augustinian than has been acknowledged" (Henry Chadwick, *Boethius: The Consolations of Music, Logic, Theology, and Philosophy* [Oxford: Clarendon Press, 1981], v). On the relation between Augustine and Boethius, see also Chadwick, 247–253. The connection between these two great figures is present symbolically in their final resting places as well: Both Augustine and Boethius are buried in San Pietro in Ciel d'Oro, in Pavia, Italy—Augustine in the sanctuary and Boethius in the crypt immediately beneath.
12. Regarding the former, Hugh Feiss, OSB, notes that, "Apart from the Bible, St. Augustine is the primary authority for Hugh's theological thinking. This is true of his theology of love and of the theologies of love of his twelfth-century successors at [the Abbey of] St. Victor" (Hugh Feiss, "General Introduction," *On Love*, 51).

read.[13] In this work, Hugh offers a detailed treatment of the liberal arts that is indebted to Augustine in various ways:

> Hugh's defense of the monastic ideal of meditative reading self-consciously looks back to Augustine's early treatment of the liberal arts curriculum. Hugh sets education in a theological and Christological context when he identifies the end of study with divine union. As for Augustine, the goal of study in the *Didascalicon* is the restoration of the soul to divine likeness; learning, as the pursuit of wisdom, is defined as an essentially religious activity. The arts are propaedeutic. . . . Hugh shares with Augustine his ambition for the curriculum that, by the study of material form and regularity, the student, properly disposed, could ascend through an ordered sequence of investigations all the way to the mind of God.[14]

*Often called "*secundus Augustinus*" ("a second Augustine"), Hugh of St. Victor was formatively influenced by Augustine's thought, both in terms of his theology in general, with its emphasis on the primacy of love, and in terms of his views on the liberal arts and their relation to philosophy and theology.*

Just as Augustine's account of the liberal arts presented them as the beginnings of a liberal education—an education ultimately ordered to a knowledge and love of God—so too does Hugh's presentation of the liberal arts see them as various ways by which

---

13. For an excellent commentary on *Didascalicon* and its striking relevance for our modern information age, see Ivan Illich, *In the Vineyard of the Text: A Commentary on Hugh's* Didascalicon (Chicago: University of Chicago Press, 1993).

14. Topping, *St. Augustine*, 116–117.

the diligent student may be led to a knowledge of higher things: first to philosophy, but ultimately to theology.

In the preface to *Didascalicon*, Hugh claims: "The things by which every man advances in knowledge are principally two—namely, reading and meditation."[15] The opening line of the first book orients all reading and all meditation to the pursuit of wisdom: "Of all things to be sought, the first is that Wisdom in which the Form of the Perfect Good stands fixed."[16] Philosophy "is the love and pursuit of Wisdom, and, in a certain way, a friendship with it";[17] it is "the discipline which investigates comprehensively the ideas of all things, human and divine."[18] Hugh continues: "In man are two things—the good and the evil, his nature and the defective state of his nature."[19] This being the case, "our entire task" is "the restoration of our nature and the removal of our deficiency."[20] The reestablishment of integrity in our nature is achieved through acquiring knowledge and virtue. For Hugh, the purpose of the arts is thus "to restore within us the divine likeness."[21] Among the arts, the seven classical liberal arts, which are also considered sciences, are the foundation for this restoration project. As Hugh argues:

> Out of all the sciences . . . the ancients, in their studies, especially selected seven to be mastered by those who were to be educated. These seven they considered so to excel all the rest in usefulness that anyone who had been thoroughly schooled in them might afterward come to a knowledge of the others by his own inquiry and effort rather than by listening to a teacher. For

15. Hugh of St. Victor, *The* Didascalicon *of Hugh of St. Victor: A Medieval Guide to the Arts*, trans. Jerome Taylor (New York: Columbia University Press, 1991), 44. Unless otherwise indicated, all *Didascalicon* quotations are from this edition.
16. Hugh of St. Victor, 1.1.
17. Hugh of St. Victor, 1.2.
18. Hugh of St. Victor, 1.4.
19. Hugh of St. Victor, 1.5.
20. Hugh of St. Victor, 1.5.
21. Hugh of St. Victor., 2.1.

> these, one might say, constitute the best instruments, the best rudiments, by which the way is prepared for the mind's complete knowledge of philosophic truth. Therefore they are called by the name tri*vium* and quadri*vium*, because by them, as by certain *ways* (*viae*), a quick mind enters into the secret places of wisdom.[22]

This account of the liberal arts, inspired by Augustine and developed by Hugh, has enjoyed a profound, enduring influence on liberal education in the Western tradition.

Thomas Aquinas

Augustine and Thomas Aquinas are undoubtedly two of the most influential thinkers in the history of Western Christianity, affecting the development of Christian philosophy and theology in myriad ways throughout the centuries. Admittedly, Augustine and Aquinas drew on quite different philosophical sources. Whereas Augustine was deeply influenced by the Neoplatonism of Plotinus and had very little access to the writings of Aristotle, Aquinas relied heavily upon the full range of Aristotle's treatises (as well as upon great Jewish and Islamic thinkers of the Middle Ages), and overall he tended to distance himself from Plato and the Neoplatonic tradition of philosophy. Furthermore, Aquinas had comparatively little direct access to Augustine's writings; instead, his knowledge of Augustine's works was through Peter Lombard's *The Sentences* and other secondary sources.

Nevertheless, his indebtedness to Augustine is widespread and manifest throughout the corpus of Aquinas.[23] One conspic-

---

22. Hugh of St. Victor, 3.3 (emphasis in the original).

23. See ed. Michael Dauphinais, Barry David, Matthew Levering, *Aquinas the Augustinian* (Washington, DC: The Catholic University of America Press, 2007). In this collection of essays, a group of scholars explores the continuities and differences between Augustine and Aquinas on such topics as the spiritual ascent to God through contemplation of the Trinity; the theology of the Word; the nature of existence, the virtues, and the fall; the image of God in man; and original sin and man's need for grace.

uous example is *De magistro* (*On the Teacher*),[24] a work bearing the same title as one of Augustine's early dialogues, in which Aquinas gives his own distinctive account of discovery (*inventio*) and learning (*disciplina*) as ways of coming to know. Aquinas is famously a disciple of Aristotle, referring to him deferentially as "the Philosopher" throughout his writings. Like Augustine before him, however, Aquinas is first and foremost a disciple of Jesus Christ. As G. K. Chesterton notes, "St. Thomas did not reconcile Christ to Aristotle; he reconciled Aristotle to Christ."[25] The truth of Chesterton's statement is evident in Aquinas's *On the Teacher*, as is his reliance upon Augustine. Even so, Aquinas does not simply follow Augustine's *De magistro* in a slavish way. Instead, he offers a synthesis that retains a version of Augustine's doctrine of illumination[26] and yet reconciles this doctrine with Aristotle's account of the role of abstraction in human knowing. Topping summarizes this synthesis as follows:

> Aquinas agrees with Augustine that it is God [who] illumines the mind through . . . universal principles. But he differs from him in ascribing a greater responsibility to the activity of the mind. First, although the knowledge of first principles is caused by God,

24. *On the Teacher* is the eleventh question in Aquinas's *Disputed Questions on Truth*, written from 1256 to 1259. Nevertheless, it is a self-contained work and has been a formative influence on recent efforts to recapture the "great tradition" of the liberal arts and liberal education. See Richard Gamble, ed., *The Great Tradition: Classical Readings on What It Means to Be an Educated Human Being* (Wilmington, DE: ISI Books, 2007), 286–298.

25. G. K. Chesterton, *Saint Thomas Aquinas: "The Dumb Ox"* (New York: Doubleday, 1956), 10.

26. Relatively little has been said in this study about Augustine's "doctrine of illumination." Although it is certainly one of the most distinctive features of his epistemology, or account of human knowing, it presents difficulties to would-be interpreters. First, scholars do not agree on what exactly Augustine intended by his doctrine of illumination. There are currently at least four distinct interpretations, all of which share the following three points in common: "(1) God is light and illumines all humans to different degrees; (2) there are intelligible truths, the *rationes aeternae*, which God illumines; and (3) human minds can know the divine truths only as God illumines them" (Ronald H. Nash, s.v. "Illumination, Divine," in *Augustine through the Ages*, 438). Second, insofar as scholars can agree on the doctrine, there is usually the impression that it must be modified in various ways in order to be viable. Aquinas's modification in his *On the Teacher* has been one of the most promising attempts to do so.

> for Aquinas, and unlike Augustine, God's illumination of the mind is mediated. . . . Illumination occurs . . . whenever the mind abstracts from images (*phantasma*). Second, Aquinas specifies how this understanding of illumination clarifies our view [of] teaching and learning. More than God's intervention is required for potential knowledge to be actualized. This something more is achieved either through the independent efforts of discovery by the student (*inventio*) or through the aid afforded by the skill of the teacher (*disciplina*).[27]

With this summary in mind, let us turn briefly to the text itself. In the first article, which is dedicated to answering the question "Can a man teach and be called a master [i.e., teacher] or God alone?" Aquinas argues:

> Just as there are two ways to be cured, one by the operation of nature alone, the other by nature as aided by medicine, so too there are two ways of acquiring science [i.e., universal knowledge], one, when natural reason by itself comes to knowledge of the unknown, and this way is called *discovery*, another when someone outside aids natural reason, and this way is called *learning*.[28]

Like Augustine, Aquinas places special emphasis on what he calls "discovery"—that is, learning a truth for oneself without the aid of an external, human teacher. Nevertheless, Aquinas does not depreciate "learning" as such: "It should be said that the manner of acquiring science through discovery is more perfect on the part of the one receiving science, insofar as he is shown to be more equipped to know, yet on the part of the one causing science

27. Topping, *St. Augustine*, 126.

28. Thomas Aquinas, "*On the Teacher*. Disputed Question on Truth, 11 (1256–1259)," in *Selected Writings on Thomas Aquinas*, ed. and trans. Ralph McInerny, Penguin Classics (New York: Penguin Books, 1998), a. 1, *resp.*

teaching is more perfect."[29] In fact, in some circumstances learning through the teaching of another can be preferable to discovery: "The one teaching, who explicitly knows the whole science, can lead us to science more expeditiously than anyone can be brought to it on his own because he foreknows the principles of the science in some generality."[30] Finally, Aquinas acknowledges with Augustine that God is the principal teacher of man:

> The light of reason by which [self-evident] principles . . . are known is placed in us by God, bringing about in us a kind of likeness of uncreated truth. Hence, since all human teaching is only efficacious because of the power of this light, it follows that it is God alone who teaches within and principally, just as nature principally and within heals.[31]

While Aquinas admits that human teachers actually teach, he agrees with Augustine that their ability to do so is rooted in the prior reality of God as "Inner Teacher."

The Liberal Arts and Liberal Education: Augustine's Relevance Today

In our own day, we stand to learn a great deal from Augustine's philosophy and theology of education. Earlier in this study, we noted that the classical way of approaching the question of happiness and the pursuit of the good life was to start with the ends and then proceed to the principles and means. By recovering a definite sense of happiness, of human

29. Aquinas, a. 2, *ad* 4.
30. Aquinas, a. 2, *ad* 4.
31. Aquinas, a. 1, *resp.*

flourishing that is grounded in our nature, we once again have a way of thinking about and pursuing education so that our learning may lead us to our ultimate good. With this end in view, we start with the liberal arts as principles or "beginnings" that direct us in various ways to higher studies. The "three ways" of grammar, logic, and rhetoric lead to foundational knowledge both of words and of human communication, thereby enabling us to pursue truth together; and the "four ways" of arithmetic, geometry, music, and astronomy lead to knowledge of basic truths about the cosmos. These humble beginnings prepare us for the study of many different disciplines and eventually philosophy, the love of wisdom, which in turn prepares us for theology, the knowledge of God.

Adopting such a well-articulated, orderly plan of liberal education is crucial if we are to regain a tradition of excellence in education for our time. As T. S. Eliot asks, "Where is the wisdom we have lost in knowledge? Where is the knowledge we have lost in information?"[32] We live in a world glutted with information and yet starving for wisdom. We have lost sight of the whole, so it should not be surprising that we do not know what to make of the parts. By recovering a robust theory and practice of liberal education, one grounded in the liberal arts that leads to philosophy and ultimately to theology, we could not only once again get our bearings, but also even reclaim the vibrant tradition of faith seeking understanding—a tradition championed by Augustine and one that has led many a student across the generations to the knowledge and love of God, who is Wisdom, Truth, and Love.

---

32. From T. S. Eliot's poem "The Rock" (1934), http://capress.link/aug0602.

By recovering a robust theory and practice of liberal education, one grounded in the liberal arts that leads to philosophy and ultimately to theology, we could not only once again get our bearings, but also even reclaim the vibrant tradition of faith seeking understanding—a tradition championed by Augustine and one that has led many a student across the generations to the knowledge and love of God, who is Wisdom, Truth, and Love.

Central to the plan laid out for us by Augustine are the moral and intellectual virtues, which he construed as various forms of love. To grow in virtue is to grow in love, and to grow in love is to move closer to the God who is Love. In Augustine's philosophy and theology of education, truth and love are central and intimately related. In order to love the truth, we must first at least in *some* sense know the truth. But then, to want to know the truth, we must be properly disposed to it—to a certain degree, we must already love it. Augustine the master teacher is aware of this delicate interplay between knowing the truth and loving the truth. His philosophy and theology of education, which has been one of the most influential in the Western tradition, is founded upon the centrality of truth and love to education. Later thinkers, such as Boethius, Hugh of St. Victor, and Thomas Aquinas, have appropriated and transformed Augustine's key contributions to education in various ways. As we look forward to the years ahead—years that seem very promising for liberal education—we would do well to allow Augustine's philosophy and theology of education to inform our own thinking on these matters.

BIBLIOGRAPHY

WORKS BY AUGUSTINE

Augustine. *Against the Academicians and the Teacher.* Indianapolis: Hackett Publishing Co., 1995.

———. *The Augustine Catechism: The Enchiridion on Faith, Hope, and Charity.* Translated by Bruce Harbert. Edited by Boniface Ramsey. Vol. 1 of *The Works of St. Augustine.* Hyde Park, NY: New City Press, 1999.

———. *City of God.* Translated by Henry Bettenson. Penguin Classics. New York: Penguin Books, 2003.

———. *The Confessions of Saint Augustine of Hippo.* Translated by Maria Boulding, OSB. Edited by David Vincent Meconi, SJ. Ignatius Critical Editions. San Francisco: Ignatius Press, 2012.

———. *Essential Sermons.* Translated by Edmund Hill, OP. Vol. 3 of *The Works of St. Augustine.* Hyde Park, NY: New City Press, 2007.

———. *Expositions of the Psalms (99–120).* Translated by Maria Boulding, OSB. Vol. 19 of *The Works of St. Augustine.* Hyde Park, NY: New City Press, 2003.

———. *Homilies on the First Epistle of John.* Translated by Boniface Ramsey. Vol. 14 of *The Works of St. Augustine.* Hyde Park, NY: New City Press, 2008.

———. *The Literal Meaning of Genesis (De Genesi ad Litteram).* Translated by John Hammond Taylor, SJ. Vols. 1 & 2, Nos. 41 & 42 of *Ancient Christian Writers: The Works of the Fathers in Translation.* New York: Paulist Press, 1982.

———. *On Free Choice of the Will.* Translated by Thomas Williams. Indianapolis: Hackett Publishing Company, 1993.

———. *On Order.* In "The Cassiciacum Dialogues of St. Augustine." Translated by Michael P. Foley. 2011 (unpublished manuscript).

———. *Revisions*. Translated by Boniface Ramsey. Vol. 2 of *The Works of St. Augustine*. Hyde Park, NY: New City Press, 2010.

———. *Teaching Christianity (De Doctrina Christiana)*. Translated by Edmund Hill, OP. Vol. 11 of *The Works of St. Augustine*. Hyde Park, NY: New City Press, 2010.

———. *Trilogy on Faith and Happiness* [*The Happy Life*, *Faith in the Unseen*, *The Advantage of Believing*]. Translated by Roland Teske, SJ, Michael G. Campbell, OSA, and Ray Kearney. Vol. 6 of *The Works of St. Augustine*. Hyde Park, NY: New City Press, 2010.

———. *The Trinity*. Translated by Edmund Hill, OP. Vol. 5 of *The Works of Saint Augustine*. Hyde Park, NY: New City Press, 2012.

Works by Other Authors

Aquinas, Thomas. "*On the Teacher*. Disputed Question on Truth, 11 (1256–1259)." In *Selected Writings of Thomas Aquinas*, edited and translated by Ralph McInerny, n.p. Penguin Classics. New York: Penguin Books, 1998.

Aristotle. *The Basic Works of Aristotle*. Edited by Richard McKeon. New York: Random House, 1941.

Boethius. *The Consolation of Philosophy*. Edited and translated by Scott Goins and Barbara H. Wyman. Ignatius Critical Editions. San Francisco: Ignatius Press, 2012.

Bowery, Anne-Marie. "Boethius." In *Augustine through the Ages: An Encyclopedia*, 108, edited by Allan D. Fitzgerald and John C. Cavadini. Grand Rapids, MI: William B. Eerdmans Publishing Co., 1999.

Brann, Eva. *What, Then, Is Time?* Lanham, MD: Rowman and Littlefield, 1999.

Brown, Peter. *Augustine of Hippo: A Biography*. Los Angeles: University of California Press, 2000.

Bussanich, John. "Happiness, Eudaimonism." In *Augustine through the Ages: An Encyclopedia*, 413–414, edited by Allan D. Fitzgerald and John C. Cavadini. Grand Rapids, MI: William B. Eerdmans Publishing Co., 1999.

Chadwick, Henry. *Boethius: The Consolations of Music, Logic, Theology, and Philosophy*. Oxford: Clarendon Press, 1981.

Chesterton, G. K. *Saint Thomas Aquinas: "The Dumb Ox."* New York: Doubleday, 1956.

Dauphinais, Michael, Barry David, Matthew Levering. *Aquinas the Augustinian*. Washington, DC: The Catholic University of America Press, 2007.

Euclid. *Elements*. Translated by Thomas L. Heath. Edited by Dana Densmore. Santa Fe, NM: Green Lion Press, 2003.

Feiss, Hugh. "General Introduction." In *On Love: A Selection of Works of Hugh, Adam, Achard, Richard, and Godfrey of St. Victor*. Edited by Hugh Feiss, OSB. Vol. 2 of *Victorine Texts in Translation: Exegesis, Theology, and Spirituality from the Abbey of St. Victor*. Hyde Park, NY: New City Press, 2012.

Fiedrowicz, Michael, and Roland Teske, SJ. "Introduction." In *Trilogy on Faith and Happiness* [Augustine's *The Happy Life, Faith in the Unseen, The Advantage of Believing*]. Translated by Roland Teske, SJ, Michael G. Campbell, OSA, and Ray Kearney. Vol. 6 of *The Works of St. Augustine*. Hyde Park, NY: New City Press, 2010.

Fitzgerald, Allan D., and John C. Cavadini, eds. *Augustine through the Ages: An Encyclopedia*. Grand Rapids, MI: William B. Eerdmans Publishing Co., 1999.

Foley, Michael P. "The Cassiciacum Dialogues of St. Augustine." 2011 (unpublished manuscript).

Fortin, Ernest L. "*Civitate Dei, De*." In *Augustine through the Ages: An Encyclopedia*, 196–202, edited by Allan D. Fitzgerald and John C. Cavadini. Grand Rapids, MI: William B. Eerdmans Publishing Co., 1999.

Gamble, Richard, ed. *The Great Tradition: Classical Readings on What It Means to Be an Educated Human Being*. Wilmington, DE: ISI Books, 2007.

Gilson, Etienne. *The Christian Philosophy of Saint Augustine*. Translated by L. E. M. Lynch. New York: Random House, 1960.

Hadot, Pierre. *Philosophy as a Way of Life: Spiritual Exercises from Socrates to Foucault*. Translated by Michael Chase. Edited by Arnold I. Davidson. Malden, MA: Blackwell Publishing, 1995.

Hermanson, Amy K., Drew M. Loewe, Kristi Schwertfeger Serrano, Lisa Michelle Thomas, and Sarah L. Yoder. "Saint Augustine and the Creation of a Distinctly Christian Rhetoric." In *The Rhetoric of St. Augustine of Hippo*: De Doctrina Christiana *and the Search for a Distinctly Christian Rhetoric*. Edited by Richard Leo Enos, et al. Waco, TX: Baylor University Press, 2008.

Hugh of St. Victor. *The* Didascalicon *of Hugh of St. Victor: A Medieval Guide to the Arts*. Translated by Jerome Taylor. New York: Columbia University Press, 1991.

Illich, Ivan. *In the Vineyard of the Text: A Commentary on Hugh's* Didascalicon. Chicago: University of Chicago Press, 1993.

Kimball, Bruce A. *Orators and Philosophers: A History of the Idea of Liberal Education*. New York: Teachers College Press, 1986.

Lehman, Jeffrey S. " 'As I read, I was set on fire': On the Psalms in Augustine's *Confessions*." *LOGOS: A Journal of Catholic Thought and Culture* 16, no. 2 (Spring 2013): 160–84.

———. "Lady Philosophy as Physician." In Boethius, *The Consolation of Philosophy*. Edited and translated by Scott Goins and Barbara H. Wyman. Ignatius Critical Editions. San Francisco: Ignatius Press, 2012.

Levering, Matthew. *The Theology of Augustine: An Introductory Guide to His Most Important Works*. Grand Rapids, MI: Baker Academic, 2013.

Lewis, C. S. *The Discarded Image: An Introduction to Medieval and Renaissance Literature*. Cambridge: Cambridge University Press, 1964.

MacIntyre, Alasdair C. *After Virtue: A Study in Moral Theory*. Notre Dame: University of Notre Dame Press, 2007.

McMahon, Robert. *Augustine's Prayerful Ascent: An Essay on the Literary Form of the* Confessions. Athens: University of Georgia Press, 1989.

———. *Understanding the Medieval Meditative Ascent: Augustine, Anselm, Boethius & Dante*. Washington, DC: The Catholic University of America Press, 2006.

McWilliam, Joanne. "*Soliloquia*." In *Augustine through the Ages: An Encyclopedia*, 806–807, edited by Allan D. Fitzgerald and John C. Cavadini. Grand Rapids, MI: William B. Eerdmans Publishing Co., 1999.

Meconi, David Vincent, SJ. *The One Christ: St. Augustine's Theology of Deification.* Washington, DC: The Catholic University of America Press, 2013.

———. *Restless Heart: The Confessions of Saint Augustine.* San Francisco: Ignatius Press, 2013.

Murphy, James J. "Foreword." In *The Rhetoric of St. Augustine of Hippo:* De Doctrina Christiana *and the Search for a Distinctly Christian Rhetoric*, edited by Richard Leo Enos, et al. Waco, TX: Baylor University Press, 2008.

Nash, Ronald H. "Illumination, Divine." In *Augustine through the Ages: An Encyclopedia*, 438–440, edited by Allan D. Fitzgerald and John C. Cavadini. Grand Rapids, MI: William B. Eerdmans Publishing Co., 1999.

O'Neill, Seamus. "Augustine and Boethius, Memory and Eternity." *Analecta Hermeneutica* 6 (2014): 1–20.

Paffenroth, Kim, and Kevin L. Hughes, eds. *Augustine and Liberal Education.* New York: Lexington Books, 2008.

Pelikan, Jaroslav. *The Emergence of the Catholic Tradition (100–600).* Vol. 1 of *The Christian Tradition: A History of the Development of Doctrine.* Chicago: University of Chicago Press, 1971.

Pollman, Karla, and Mark Vessey, eds. *Augustine and the Disciplines: From Cassiciacum to* Confessions. New York: Oxford University Press, 2005.

Possidius. *The Life of St. Augustine: A Translation of the* Sancti Augustini Vita *by Possidius, Bishop of Calama.* Translated by Herbert T. Weiskotten. Vol. 6 of *Christian Roman Empire Series.* Merchantville, NJ: Evolution Publishing, 2008.

Schiavo, Anthony P., Jr. "Preface to the 2008 Edition." In Possidius, *The Life of St. Augustine: A Translation of the* Sancti Augustini Vita *by Possidius, Bishop of Calama.* Translated by Herbert T. Weiskotten. Vol. 6 of *Christian Roman Empire Series.* Merchantville, NJ: Evolution Publishing, 2008.

Stark, Rodney. *The Rise of Christianity: A Sociologist Reconsiders History.* Princeton: Princeton University Press, 1996.

Stock, Brian. *Augustine the Reader: Meditation, Self-Knowledge, and the Ethics of Interpretation.* Cambridge: Harvard University Press, 1996.

———. *Augustine's Inner Dialogue: Philosophical Soliloquy in Late Antiquity*. New York: Cambridge University Press, 2010.

Topping, Ryan N. S. *Happiness and Wisdom: Augustine's Early Theology of Education*. Washington, DC: The Catholic University of America Press, 2012.

———. *St. Augustine. Continuum Library of Educational Thought*. New York: Continuum International Publishing Group, 2010.

Van Bavel, Tarsicius J., OSA. "Love." In *Augustine through the Ages: An Encyclopedia*, 509–516, edited by Allan D. Fitzgerald and John C. Cavadini. Grand Rapids, MI: William B. Eerdmans Publishing Co., 1999.

Questions for Discussion

1. What kind of education did Augustine receive? What was the generally accepted purpose of studying the liberal arts, especially rhetoric? What influence did Augustine's mother have on him? His father? How, if at all, did their influence on Augustine change over time?

2. What change occurred in Augustine when he read Cicero's *Hortensius*? Why did Augustine fall in with the Manichees? What influence did Ambrose have on Augustine? What did Augustine find in the books of the Platonists?

3. What was the "Great Persecution," and how did it affect Christianity in North Africa? Who were the Donatists, and why did Augustine object to their claims regarding the clergy, ordination, and baptism?

4. What are the two distinct schools of thought on the nature and purpose of education in the Western tradition? What was Augustine's stance vis-à-vis these schools? Following Augustine's conversion, what became the most significant influence on his philosophy and theology of education?

5. For Augustine, what is the ultimate purpose of education? How, if at all, do his views on happiness change over the course of his life (as far as we can tell from his writings)? What view of education does Augustine champion in his Cassiciacum dialogues? What is the place of God and divine assistance in these dialogues?

6. What account does Augustine give of the liberal arts? What part do they play in a liberal education? What is the image of tiles in a mosaic meant to illustrate? Did Augustine's views on the liberal arts change as he matured? If so, how? What role did the liberal arts play in Augustine's own intellectual and moral journey toward God?

7. How exactly is love a "master theme" for Augustine's theology? How does love inform his philosophy and theology of education? How does each of his four major works—*Confessions*, *City of God*, *On the Trinity*, and *On Christian Teaching*—shed light on Augustine's work as a master teacher?

8. In what ways did Augustine influence the thought of such major figures as Boethius, Hugh of St. Victor, and Thomas Aquinas? To what extent is the Western tradition of the liberal arts and liberal education indebted to Augustine and his students?

9. What relevance might Augustine's philosophy and theology of education have for us today? How could Augustine's vision of education help guide those committed to classical Christian education?

About the Author

Jeffrey S. Lehman is Professor of Humanities, Director of the Graduate Program in Classical Education, and Director of the St. Augustine Center for Catholic Liberal Education and Culture at the University of Dallas. He holds a BA in biblical literature and philosophy from Taylor University in Upland, IN; an MA in philosophy of religion and ethics from Biola University in La Mirada, CA; and an MA and PhD in philosophy from the University of Dallas in Irving, TX. Among his publications are the monograph *Socratic Conversation: Bringing the Dialogues of Plato and the Socratic Tradition into Today's Classroom* (published by Classical Academic Press), an introductory text and reader in primary sources on the liberal art of logic, and various articles on Plato, Aristotle, Vergil, Augustine, Boethius, and Thomas More. Lehman has served as a founding fellow of the Center for Thomas Mores Studies, a Justin Martyr Fellow of the Institute for Catholic Liberal Education, a fellow of the Great Hearts Institute for Classical Education, and the founding director of Arts of Liberty (artsofliberty.udallas.edu), an online compendium of resources whose aim is to educate students, teachers, and lifelong learners in the purpose and power of the liberal arts and liberal education. He has also served as headmaster of Fieldstead Academy, where he crafted a 7–12 integrated classical Christian curriculum, including the study of Greek and Latin as well as great works of the Western tradition from across the disciplines. Lehman has studied, taught, and delivered public lectures around the country and internationally.